PRAISE FOR THE
FUSSY EATER REBOOT

"If you want to set your children up for a healthy relationship with food, this is the book for you. Marie-France takes the pressure off parents, sets children up for success, and brings joy back to mealtimes."

Amelia Phillips, Nutritionist and host of Healthy Her

"Marie-France's work is grounded in evidence, experience, and deep compassion. This book is a balm for parents navigating fussy eating, offering practical, achievable ways to create calm and connection at the table."

Madeleine Morris, author of Guilt-Free Bottle Feeding

"Marie-France transformed the way our family approaches food. What was once stressful is now calm, connected, and full of progress."

Renee K., mum of two

"Mealtimes used to end in tears. Now we slow down, reconnect, and actually enjoy food together."

Natalie P., mum of two

"The approach worked. My son now confidently tries new foods, and mealtimes are a pleasure again."

Michelle X., mum of three

"Her approach restored calm and structure to our table. Mealtimes feel like family time again."

Stef S., mum of two

THE FUSSY EATER REBOOT

CONFIDENT EATING: A PARENTING PLAN FOR STUBBORN PICKY EATERS

MARIE-FRANCE LAVAL

Copyright © 2026 by Marie-France Laval

All rights reserved.

No part of this publication may be reproduced, stored in a retrieval system, distributed, or transmitted in any form or by any means, including electronic, mechanical, photocopying, recording, or otherwise, without the prior written permission of the publisher, except in the case of brief quotations used in reviews or scholarly works.

This book may not be used, reproduced, or transmitted in whole or in part for the purposes of training artificial intelligence systems, machine learning models, or similar technologies without explicit written permission from the copyright holder.

The information in this book is intended for general educational purposes only and is not a substitute for professional medical, psychological, or nutritional advice. Readers should consult a qualified professional regarding any concerns about their child's health, development, or wellbeing.

The author has made every effort to ensure the accuracy of the information contained in this book. However, no responsibility can be accepted for any errors or omissions, or for any outcomes arising from the use of the information provided.

All names and identifying details have been changed to protect the privacy of individuals.

First published in 2026

ISBN: 978-1-7645255-1-0

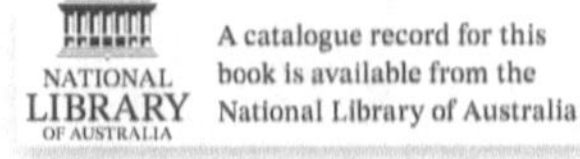

CONTENTS

THE FUSSY EATER REBOOT

Confident Eating: A Parenting Plan for Stubborn Picky Eaters

ACKNOWLEDGMENTS

To my sister Nathalie, whose experience of olfactory hypersensitivity I remember to this day.

To my husband and children, for their patience, curiosity, and steady support, and for the many meals you cook while I work evenings with families.

To my ally and mentor, Daniel, whose wisdom and encouragement have carried me further than I could have gone alone.

And most of all, to the many parents and children I have had the privilege of meeting along the way. Thank you for trusting me with your stories. I have learned far more from you, and from your devotion and courage, than I could ever hope to offer in return.

INTRODUCTION

It's dinner time again. You set your child's plate down, holding your breath, just for a moment. Before the fork even touches the food, the battle begins. 'I'm not eating that!' Your stubborn child's face scrunches up in defiance, and you feel the familiar wave of frustration.

For many parents, the dread starts long before the meal itself–that pit in the stomach, knowing another struggle is coming. It's easy to feel overwhelmed, guilty, or even ashamed when mealtimes spiral out of control.

But there is another way forward. This book offers a gentle, practical roadmap to help your child overcome fussy eating–and to help you rediscover calm, confidence, and connection at the table.

How this book works

The heart of this book is the approach–five step-by-step resets that bring calm, rebuild trust, and help your child grow confident around food. Each Reboot is practical, doable, and designed to fit real family life.

Here's the journey you'll take:

- **Reboot 1**: Building the foundations for calm eating
- **Reboot 2**: Sharing power without losing your role
- **Reboot 3**: From refusal to familiarity
- **Reboot 4**: What you say matters more than you think
- **Reboot 5**: Turning ideas into everyday meals

By the time you complete these five Reboots, feeding will no longer feel like something you're constantly trying to get right. You'll understand what your child needs, how to respond when challenges arise, and how to support their eating as they grow. You won't need to hold your breath at mealtimes–you'll have a clear, steady way forward.

WHAT WE CALL FUSSY EATING–AND WHY IT VARIES SO MUCH

Fussy eating is common but it's rarely simple. There's no single, agreed definition, and the term is often used to describe a wide range of eating behaviours.

Some children show strong preferences, refuse new foods, or stick to only a few 'safe' options. For others, the difficulties are more extreme, narrowing their diet and affecting overall nutrition and family life.

Parents often notice patterns emerging over time. A child may refuse a food the moment they see it. This might be because of the food itself, how it looks, the way items are touching, or a strong reaction to certain textures or smells.

Understanding what drives these reactions is the first step toward meaningful change.

WHO THIS BOOK IS FOR

You picked up this book because you want to help your child eat better and develop a healthy relationship with food. You've likely tried everything you can–preparing familiar meals, avoiding conflict, even bargaining at times. Beneath it all is the hope that your child can feel more at ease around food over time.

We've all heard advice like:

- 'All kids are fussy, they grow out of it.'
- 'Just starve them, they'll eat when they're hungry.'
- 'You're overreacting, just relax.'

Yet, your child's eating habits still feel different. Maybe they:

- eat only a handful of foods and reject anything new
- skip meals rather than eat unfamiliar or disliked foods
- have mealtime meltdowns, gag, or struggle in social eating situations
- need distractions (like screens) just to eat

If this sounds familiar, you're not alone. Many parents have been where you are, and have discovered that progress is possible.

This book was written with parents like you in mind. It is for families with children up to 12 years old, whether your child is typically developing, has additional needs such as autism or ADHD, or experiences sensory sensitivities. It's for those who feel stuck, overwhelmed, or out of options, and who want a long-term, sustainable approach rather than another quick fix to 'get kids to eat'.

How this book helps

This book isn't about fixing your child. It's about understanding their unique relationship with food and shaping an environment where they can thrive. This book will help you gain clarity and empathy for why your child struggles with food. From there, you'll learn how to parent in ways that remove pressure, build trust, and foster curiosity, so your child can begin exploring new foods on their own terms.

A note on the stories in this book

Each example in this book reflects the real experiences of families I've had the honour of working alongside. To protect privacy, I've changed names and identifying details and combined or adapted some examples. They're not case studies in the clinical sense, but illustrations of how fussy eating looks in everyday family life.

HOW TO USE THIS BOOK

I'm on your team, and this book is here to support rather than overwhelm you.

Start by reading it all the way through; the early sections will help you see where you and your child are right now, reduce the pressure you put on yourself, and understand your child's challenges with empathy.

Then, turn to the Reboots. These are the step-by-step strategies you'll use at home. Each Reboot builds on the last. Following them in order will give you and your child the best chance to make steady, confident progress.

By the end, you'll have a structured plan of action to guide your family from mealtime battles to calmer, more connected dining–and a child who feels empowered to explore food in a way that works for them.

Reflection & Progress Tracking

Along the way, you'll be encouraged to reflect on your child's progress, especially as you move through the five Reboot stages. Each stage helps you notice subtle shifts–a calmer table, more relaxed mealtimes, and a growing sense of ease at mealtimes and within your family.

ABOUT THE AUTHOR

I'm Marie-France Laval, the founder and CEO of Fussy Eater Solutions. I began running workshops for parents in 2009, believing I understood fussy eating. It wasn't until I worked more closely with families that I saw the full range and complexity of feeding challenges.

Since 2017, through *Fussy Eater Solutions*, I've focused entirely on helping families navigate the challenges of extreme fussy eating.

Over the years, I've supported families whose children experience feeding difficulties–including those with autism, ADHD, ARFID, choking phobias, or medical conditions affecting eating.

My approach combines knowledge and empathy with a deep understanding of behaviour and emotion. I first trained in counselling and social work in France before becoming a qualified Dietitian-Nutritionist. My curiosity about the fear and anxiety that food can evoke led me to study Clinical Hypnotherapy and Psychotherapy. Today, I draw on all these experiences to help families with care, evidence, and insight.

Through my business, I've worked with hundreds of families, presented to key organisations, and contributed to media discussions on fussy eating, including features for ABC, SBS, and The Age Newspaper.

I wrote this book to share an approach that helps families find peace at the table. It's hard to watch children struggle with eating when it is fundamentally part of learning and growing. When we act early, we can often prevent feeding difficulties from becoming long-term struggles.

Even children with significant feeding challenges, including sensory sensitivities or long-standing fear around food, can learn to feel safer, more capable, and sometimes even find enjoyment with food over time. I hope this book helps you replace frustration with calm, and fear with curiosity, so that mealtimes feel more connected, relaxed, and supportive.

This work is also personal for me.

When my children were young, mealtimes at home often felt tense. I worried about what to cook and how the children would react. There were no dramatic scenes, just a steady undercurrent of stress, the sense that dinner was something to brace myself for.

By contrast, our eating experience on holiday in France was starkly different. Surrounded by family, my children joined conversations, helped themselves to food, and ate with ease. I didn't always know exactly what they ate, but I knew they were fine. Meals felt light, social, and joyful.

What the French call *convivialité*–the pleasure of sharing a meal– was the essential ingredient!

That experience taught me something lasting: when mealtimes feel relaxed and social, both children and parents (re)gain a sense of safety and ease. And when the atmosphere changes, eating changes.

Thank you for joining me as we begin your family's food Reboot!

CHAPTER 1
LET'S GET TO KNOW EACH OTHER

Despite the diversity of families and the uniqueness of each child, we all face a common challenge: navigating food, feeding, and mealtimes. As you read this chapter, you may recognise your child or yourself.

IS THIS YOU?

Parenting children at mealtimes is tough. The cycle repeats: school pickups, activities, exhaustion, then the battle over food. You cook, you clean, and tomorrow it starts again.

This routine is played out day after day, year after year. It adds up to thousands of meals and takes a toll on our energy, patience and perhaps even our motivation.

Do any of these thoughts sound familiar?

- 'I feel inadequate when I see other children eating everything while my child refuses.'
- 'People judge me, assuming I'm trying too hard or not trying hard enough.'
- 'Mealtimes are exhausting and always end in frustration.'

- 'I've tried everything–hiding vegetables, offering rewards, even punishments–but nothing works.'
- 'I worry my child will never eat like everyone else.'

If you are nodding in recognition, just know that given the right environment, your child can overcome fussy eating of their own volition.

IS THIS YOUR CHILD?

Fussy eating can take different forms at different ages. Here's what it may look like:

Toddlers & Preschoolers (1–4 years)

- Will (1) refuses all new foods, no matter how they're offered
- Lily (3) can only eat if distracted by a screen or toy

School-Age Children (5–7 years)

- Jess (5) refuses food before even tasting it, saying 'yuck' at every meal
- Jasper (7) gags or spits out foods with certain textures, even if he used to eat them before

Older Children (8+ years)

- Sophie (11) avoids eating at birthday parties or sleepovers because she's afraid of unfamiliar food

Each of these children has distinct challenges, but the common thread is anxiety or discomfort around food. The good news? With the right approach, all of them can learn to eat with confidence.

Every child is unique, and the way they express their fussy-eating challenges can be just as individual. Whether or not your child's behaviour resembles any of the children above, you can learn to support them effectively, leading them to overcome their fussy eating so mealtimes can become a source of joy, rather than frustration.

MEET ME WHERE I MEET YOU

Parenting a child who struggles with food can feel lonely. You've tried everything you can, and yet mealtimes still feel tense. I know that exhaustion–the endless cycle of trying, hoping, and wondering what you've missed.

While I may not have met you personally, I've worked with many families just like yours, through mealtime video analyses, home visits, and heartfelt conversations with parents. I've seen the patterns, the tears, and the breakthroughs. And I've seen how calm can replace fear and how peace can slowly return to the table.

My role is to meet you exactly where you are–in the worry and the fierce devotion that keeps you trying. Together, we'll explore what's happening beneath the surface of your child's eating, rebuild confidence at your table, and rediscover calm, one small step at a time.

So, take a breath. You don't need to have it all figured out. You've already begun the Reboot–simply by showing up.

SECTION 1: CUT YOURSELF SOME SLACK

Before we change anything, we need a clearer picture of what's happening–and some compassion for the fact that feeding challenges affect the whole family. This section helps you take stock without blame: what fussy eating looks like in your home, when it began, and what tends to trigger it. Then we'll focus on you–because you're part of this feeding journey too. The calmer and more supported you feel, the easier it becomes to help your child feel safe, steady, and ready to learn.

CHAPTER 2

THE PRESENTATION OF FUSSY EATING IN YOUR FAMILY

This chapter helps you take a closer look at how fussy eating presents in your family, and when it first became a concern.

WHEN DID FUSSY EATING START?

Fussy eating often begins in early childhood. Many adults who were fussy eaters as children recall their struggles starting when they were young.[1] Take a moment to think back–how young was *young* in your family?

Babies who showed early feeding difficulties

Early feeding challenges can shape how children learn to eat and how comfortable they feel around food and at mealtimes.[2] Children can develop negative associations from these early experiences. A common one is spoon aversion, where a child enters *fight, flight, or freeze* responses when faced with a feeding spoon.

Baby Allegra, at ten months old, screamed the moment her parents brought out her bib. She would cry at any

attempt to fit it on, so they often gave up and left the bib on the chair. Eventually, they managed to put her in her highchair using distractions, but as soon as she saw the spoon, she arched her body and kicked her legs. Mum would try to sneak a spoonful of purée into Allegra's mouth, who usually spat it out, crying profusely. It turned out Allegra had suffered from severe reflux for about four months and associated feeding with pain.

If any of this sounds familiar, think back to whether these difficulties were discussed with your GP or child health nurse. Did your child see an allergist, gastroenterologist, lactation consultant, or speech pathologist for further assessment?

If so, it's worth holding this in mind as you read on. Your child may have been working hard around food for a long time. When early feeding is difficult, the learning-to-eat journey can be interrupted before it has a chance to unfold, and mealtimes can become more about coping rather than learning.

Toddlers and beyond

Some children who previously ate a wide range of foods begin to refuse new or unfamiliar foods during toddlerhood. This is often part of a typical developmental phase known as food neophobia, which we'll discuss later in the book. For these children, eating usually continues to progress with time and support.

For other children in that same age group, food neophobia may become compounded if physical discomfort or heightened anxiety comes into play. These children may appear more stubborn or rigid around food, along with greater sensitivity to texture, taste, or appearance than their peers.

Feeding may turn into a 'hit-and-miss' experience–one day they enjoy a meal, the next they refuse it completely. Many parents can pinpoint the exact moment broccoli went from acceptable to deeply offensive.

> Samuel's mother used to count herself lucky because he ate everything. He was always happy and excited to sit down for meals. It all changed when Samuel turned two. He started complaining about food with his favourite dinnertime comments being 'It's yuck' and 'I don't like it'.

WHAT DOES FUSSY EATING LOOK LIKE IN YOUR FAMILY?

Fussy eating can appear in different ways, and your child may show one or more of these behaviours at different times.

'Misbehaving' at mealtime

For some families, mealtimes involve resistance from the very beginning. A child may avoid coming to the table or run away after seeing the food on their plate.

At the table, children may argue that food is 'yuck', push it away or ask for something else to eat. They may nibble briefly before declaring they are full, even though hunger returns soon after.

When encouraged to eat, distress may escalate into tantrums or meltdowns. Parents often try reasoning, negotiating, or offering rewards, only to find that nothing seems to help.

Eating better at childcare

Some children eat better at childcare than at home, even when offered complex, mixed foods.

They may be compartmentalising how they eat–accepting certain foods in specific settings. They may also benefit from the influence of their peers.[3]

Either way, this is encouraging. Eating well at childcare shows that your child can eat these foods. From an oral-motor perspective (chewing and swallowing) and a sensory perspective (taste, smell, and noise), this can be reassuring.

You may try to recreate childcare meals at home, but many parents find their child does not respond in the same way. From your child's point of view, the context is simply different.

> When Sophia heard that three-year-old Ed ate tuna bake at childcare, she was amazed. A few weeks later, the staff even took a picture of Ed happily eating the pasta dish. Intrigued, Sophia asked for the recipe. She even bought the same cheese and pasta brands–yet Ed refused to eat the bake when she prepared it at home.

Struggling to eat away from homes

These children may come back from childcare or school having eaten very little, or nothing at all.

Factors such as the environment–including noise, smells, and other distractions–can be overwhelming, making it harder to cope with the complex, mixed foods often served in childcare settings, or even familiar foods packed in a lunchbox. As a result, a child may come home hungry, irritated, exhausted, and anxious about what food will be offered next.

As children get older, some begin to avoid restaurants, birthday parties, school camps, or sleepovers, worrying that they won't be able to eat anything. Parents may find themselves having to explain their child's feeding challenges to other parents, teachers, or even restaurant staff.

All children need support to develop the skills required to eat away from home. Without support, difficulties in this area can persist and, for some children, become more entrenched over time.

> Jackson's parents say they never eat out anymore with him because the last time they did, the ten-year-old refused everything–including chips. He also would not sit, so his parents could not eat their own meals in peace. Once back in the car, Jackson had a massive meltdown because 'there was nothing he could eat there'. When

going to family events, Jackson's parents have now resorted to bringing a lunch box so he has something he can eat.

Children with special needs

Your child may struggle with eating due to their developmental profile, special health condition, or a specific diagnosis, and may require more specialised support.

Children on the autism spectrum and/or with ADHD often experience unique challenges with eating.

 Research suggests that while around 25–35% of typically developing children display fussy or selective eating, this rises sharply in autism, where up to 88% of children show limited food preferences.[4,5]

They may be highly selective or fixated on certain foods based on colour, texture, or presentation, as sensory sensitivities may trigger threat responses. The eating environment can also be overwhelming, bright lights, background noise, or even eating in front of others may feel uncomfortable or distressing, making it harder for them to manage mealtimes comfortably.

For children with ADHD, mealtimes may present additional challenges. They may struggle to sit still, have a reduced appetite due to medication, or find it difficult to relax enough to recognise hunger cues.

In this chapter, you've begun to recognise how fussy eating shows up in your family–when it started, how it has evolved, and what patterns it follows.

In the next chapter, we'll turn the focus to you and the emotions that arise when feeding your child. We'll explore the pressures, guilt, and self-doubt that build over time, and how easing that weight helps you show up with more calm and compassion for both yourself and your child.

CHAPTER 3
PRESSURES, EMOTIONS, AND CO-REGULATION WITH YOUR CHILD

Over the years, I've watched more family dinners than I can count. If there were an Olympic event for observing mealtimes, I'd be well qualified to commentate.

You've already seen much of this in your own home. Children refusing food they ate yesterday, plates pushed away with the familiar cry of 'yuck'. None of it will feel new.

What often goes unnoticed is everything else happening in the frame. In those moments, it isn't only the child who is responding. Parents are there too, watching, waiting, encouraging, worrying, adjusting. Feeding doesn't happen in isolation; it unfolds between people.

This chapter steps back to look at the whole scene. Not just the child refusing food, but the parent beside them, managing their own reactions in real time. It's the beginning of understanding feeding as a shared process, where emotions and pressures pass between child and parent and influence their ability to co-regulate.

As you read, you're not being asked to change anything yet. This chapter is about noticing what's already there, so you can see the bigger picture more clearly.

EXTERNAL AND INTERNAL PRESSURES

Feeding a child can stir up pressure from every direction–friends, family, professionals, even your own inner voice. Some of these pressures are external; others are deeply internal. Both can leave you questioning yourself and your parenting. Let's start by looking at where these pressures come from and how they shape your confidence at mealtimes.

Confusing advice

People often describe fussy eating as a 'normal phase' that most children go through. However, even professionals can struggle to distinguish between typical fussy eating and more serious feeding challenges. Because many children with feeding difficulties still grow well, parents are often told to simply wait it out.

Family and friends, too, may not know how to offer meaningful support. They might share what worked for them, without realising that every child's journey is different. Some might even suggest extreme measures, such as 'starving' children or forcing them to eat.

Social media adds to the confusion, with endless posts about perfectly balanced lunchboxes and creative food displays. You may feel pressured to become your child's feeding therapist, exhausting yourself at mealtimes as you try to convince them to bite into a cucumber.

Judgemental comments

At a recent birthday party, one of my clients experienced an unsettling moment when a stranger commented on her daughter's size, saying, 'She's so skinny. She needs to eat more.'

This kind of uninvited remark can leave parents feeling shaken and exposed. Even well-meaning family members can add pressure without realising it. Grandparents, for example, may say, 'In my day, you ate what you were given,' or 'You just need to be firmer.'

Remarks like these often linger, shaping how parents feel at the table and adding to the emotional weight of mealtimes.

Mother-blaming

It's an unfortunate reality that mothers are often blamed when something 'goes wrong' with their child, including fussy eating.

Blaming mothers for a child's behaviour is not a new phenomenon. In the 1940s, Austrian physician Leo Kanner incorrectly theorised that a lack of maternal warmth caused autism, a belief later disproved by science.[1] Despite this, studies show that mothers continue to experience stigma and often blame themselves for their child's autism.[2]

Mother-blaming is deeply embedded in our culture, so it can show up quietly in all of us, in the way we judge ourselves and sometimes each other against impossible standards. Naming this pattern helps us move toward compassion instead of judgement.

Nutritional pressures

As a parent of a fussy eater, you may worry about their nutrition and how it could affect them both now and in the future. A 2022 survey found that 83% of parents shared similar worries about their children not getting the right nutrients due to selective eating habits.[3]

These worries don't arise in a vacuum, they're shaped by the culture around you. In many Anglo-Saxon societies, eating is influenced by what sociologist Claude Fischler called *nutritionism*: the belief that food's main purpose is to deliver micro- and macronutrients. It's common to hear 'Food is fuel', as if eating were simply refuelling a machine rather than sharing a meal. This mindset narrows our view of eating, turning it into a technical task centred on nutrients, calories, and control.

Even if you don't consciously think this way, you're surrounded by messages that promote it–in the media, on packaging, and even through school lunchbox scrutiny. Practically, this shows up in how food is served: each child's meal is pre-plated, monitored, and judged separately. And at the end of the meal, what's left behind becomes visible evidence and another reason to worry–the untouched broccoli staring up from the plate like a report card. This is a *tree-based* approach to food, where each bite or nutrient is judged on its own, rather than the *forest*–the broader experience of shared meals, connection, and gradual exposure to a variety of foods.

In the French approach, the focus is on the forest–the shared experience, the conversation, and the food variety that builds nutrition over time. At the start of the meal, food is placed in the centre of the table, and everyone, including children, begin with an empty plate and then help themselves. At the end of the meal, no one knows–or needs to know–exactly what or how much each person ate. The focus is on having a satisfying experience, so that one feels good that as they have eaten enough.

When mealtimes are shaped by a 'fuel mindset', even subtly, feeding can start to feel like a test you're responsible for passing. This pressure is cultural rather than personal, which helps explain why so many parents feel anxious.

Personal challenges with food

Your own relationship with food and body image can shape how you feed your child–often more than you realise. Past experiences, whether with fussy eating, dieting, disordered eating, or food-related shame, may quietly influence what you serve, how you respond, or how much pressure you feel to 'get it right'.

As Becky delves into her child's fussy eating challenges, a torrent of tears suddenly overtakes her. Growing up, she was punished 'being difficult to feed' and still carries strong food aversions today. Now, supporting her son, those memories resurface, stirring sadness, self-doubt, and worry about repeating old patterns.

Parenting styles at the dinner table

Parents don't always agree on how to manage fussy eating. As one mother told me, 'My child's extreme fussy eating almost cost me my marriage.'

Differences in beliefs, stress levels, and parenting styles can easily spill into mealtimes. Most parents understand the importance of presenting a united front, yet this can be difficult when emotions run high and opinions differ about what's best.

Parenting styles influence how boundaries are set, how much flexibility is offered, and how much pressure is applied. At the dinner table, these differences become especially visible. They shape not only what happens during a meal, but the emotional tone of that space.

Broadly speaking, three parenting styles tend to show up around food: authoritarian, indulgent, and authoritative.

> Jeff and Sally are the parents of two selective eaters. Jeff wrestles with concerns about the children's nutrition, and attempts to ensure they eat by negotiating the number of spoonfuls they must consume at each meal. Sally, on the other hand, questions how far the punitive measures or threats need to escalate before Jeff recognises that the children are developing an aversion to certain foods. Thus, a rift in their approaches is emerging.

Authoritarian

I once sat at dinner with a family whose father had an authoritarian parenting style. I vividly remember this meal—he expected his children to sit and comply with his many requests. His intimidating demeanour left me profoundly uneasy.

The authoritarian parenting style is highly controlling, demanding obedience at all costs. Authoritarian parents may attempt to control their child's eating by insisting they eat certain foods while restricting access to others, often based on their own preferences and beliefs about nutrition. In many ways, it's a parent-centred feeding style rather than a child-centred one. It often backfires, leading to issues such as a lower intake of fruit and vegetables.[4]

Authoritarian parents may believe they are winning the fussy-eating battle–but this is usually short-lived. The compliant child may attempt to swallow the offending food, only to gag or vomit because, clearly, their body disagrees.

Indulgent

Indulgent parenting takes the opposite approach. I often meet families who give their children considerable freedom and little structure at mealtimes, serving only the foods their child will eat.

While this may feel liberating, indulgent parenting hands the menu over to children who, developmentally speaking, have close to zero expertise in food. Unsurprisingly, they stick with what feels safest and most familiar.

At first, accommodation can appear helpful, reducing conflict and making meals feel more peaceful. Children miss out on the exposure they need to new foods and learn, often unintentionally, that avoidance reduces their discomfort.

> Amy has served dinner to her five-year-old twins, Ava and Juliette. Juliette complains and requests chicken nuggets instead of the roast chicken Amy served. Then Ava joins in. Amy switches to short-order cooking mode, following the children's instructions and serving them chicken nuggets and chips.

Authoritative

In contrast to authoritarian and indulgent parenting styles, a balanced approach known as authoritative parenting offers firm boundaries alongside emotional support and nurturing. This style is widely regarded as highly effective.

In the families I work with, we aim to balance structure with flexibility at mealtimes. For example, children are expected to sit properly during the meal but are also encouraged to feel relaxed and happy, without pressure to eat any particular food. This balanced approach helps foster a positive relationship with food.

The authoritative parenting style aligns closely with the philosophy of this book. It emphasises the importance of setting boundaries while also respecting the child's autonomy and emotions.

 As Rose sets the food on the table using our Mealtime System, her children understand the routine. They know they are expected to sit properly and politely choose their food options. The children relax because they know they always find something they can eat in the selection. They have the freedom to make choices and feel empowered to feed themselves.

What if my parenting style doesn't match my partner's?

When partners approach mealtimes differently, the contrast can create confusion for children. They may receive mixed messages about expectations, which can heighten anxiety and resistance.

Also, parents may feel undermined or frustrated when their partner does not mirror their efforts. Mealtimes may become emotionally charged as each parent tries to manage the situation in their own way.

Children quickly sense these differences. Some may even test boundaries by aligning with one parent or switching sides depending on the moment, further straining the dynamic.

Differing parenting styles don't just shape what happens at the table–they shape how calm, consistent, or tense that space feels for everyone.

When I work with parents, my aim is to bring them onto the same page with a shared plan they both feel confident using. But sometimes one parent is the primary driver of change–the one reading, learning, and putting the strategies into practice. If that's you, take heart: your consistency still makes a meaningful difference. Children benefit enormously from even *one* calm, predictable, pressure-free adult at the table.

And often, when the other parent or other carers see the positive shift–fewer battles, less tension, a calmer child–they naturally start to align. Change has a way of pulling people in when they can feel the difference.

Family trauma

Many families start their feeding journey while carrying emotional wounds that run deeper than mealtimes. Experiences such as prolonged medical stress, complicated births, or caring for a seriously ill family member can affect the entire household. For some parents, this includes profound losses or long periods in hospital–situations that naturally shape how they approach safety, nourishment, and their child's wellbeing.

Trauma doesn't need to be dramatic to matter. Any prolonged stress can influence how parents feed, protect, or respond to their child. Naming this context isn't about comparison–it's about compassion. Understanding your family's experiences can help explain why feeding feels so emotional, and why certain patterns are hard to shift.

Some describe being in 'therapy mode' all the time–adjusting routines, avoiding triggers, and working tirelessly to keep things calm. Mealtimes, like much of daily life, can reflect that same state of alertness.

These families aren't failing–they are surviving. When the nervous system is in survival mode, structure naturally gives way to coping. Meals may become simple, repetitive, or irregular.

The next section invites you to pause and gently reflect on how these pressures may be showing up for you.

EMOTIONS

All the pressures we've explored so far–the daily ones and the deeper, ongoing stresses–feed into the emotions you feel around food and mealtimes. These emotions don't exist in isolation; they interact, overlap, and often amplify one another.

Like many parents, you may find that frustration, worry, or guilt surface again and again.

The graphic below gives you a visual snapshot of the key emotions parents often experience at mealtimes. As you read through them, take a moment to rate each one out of 10–with 10 being the strongest or most concerning–so you can identify which feelings need your attention most.

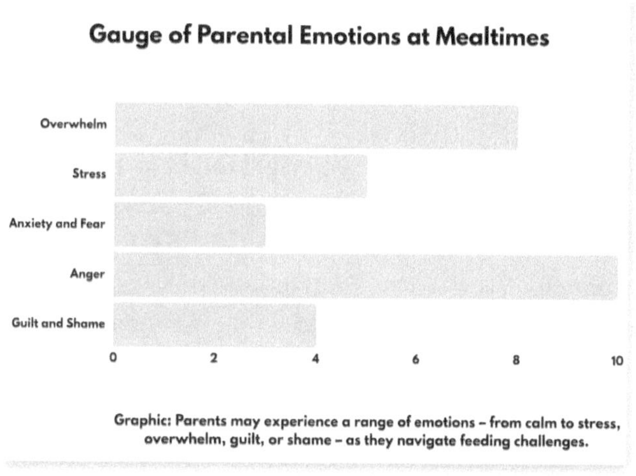

Gauge of Parental Emotions at Mealtimes

Graphic: Parents may experience a range of emotions – from calm to stress, overwhelm, guilt, or shame – as they navigate feeding challenges.

Overwhelm

Do you ever feel like the demands on you just keep growing? Between work, family, school runs, and daily routines, it can feel as though there's never enough time or energy to go around. Even something as simple as planning dinner can become another task on an already crowded list and feel impossible. Perhaps you no longer know what to serve. You know your usual food won't work for your fussy eater, and they refuse most of what you put on their plate.

On a scale of 0 to 10, how overwhelmed do you feel?

Stress

Do you feel tense at mealtimes? Does your heart race, your chest tighten, or your patience wear thin? Do you find it hard to relax and enjoy a meal with your family?

When stress takes over, mealtimes can feel like a test of endurance. You may notice yourself reacting–speaking sharply or feeling irritated as tension builds.

Take a moment to notice where stress shows up in your body. How often does it appear, and what seems to trigger it? Stress is often easier to ease once it's been named. On a scale of 0 to 10, how would you rate your stress at mealtimes?

Fear

Are you constantly worried that your child might go hungry, miss out on essential nutrients, or experience long-term effects on growth and health? Concerns like these can make fear grow quietly in the background.

Some parents also worry that unless they remind, prompt, or persuade their child to eat, their child won't eat enough.

Societal expectations and feeding norms often intensify these worries. You may find yourself comparing your child's eating habits to others or wondering whether fussy eating will persist into adulthood, affecting their wellbeing and relationship with food.

On a scale of 0 to 10, how strong is your worry about your child's eating–both the variety and the amount?

Anxiety

If fear is about what's happening right now, anxiety is about what might happen next.

Do you notice a familiar knot in your stomach as mealtime approaches? Do you find yourself thinking, 'What if they refuse again? What if they gag? What if they choke? What if tonight ends in another meltdown?'

Anxiety thrives on these 'what ifs'; building anticipation before the plate even reaches the table.

Sometimes, anxiety leads you to play it safe too–avoiding foods your child might reject or accommodating their preferences to prevent distress for both you and your child. These strategies can bring short-term relief, helping to ease *your own* anxiety, but the underlying unease remains.

Anger

Do you find yourself getting angry with your fussy eater? Does your frustration sometimes extend to your partner–when they don't help or disagree with your approach? Does your child's eating 'drive you mad'? Do you ever reach breaking point, argue with your child, or leave the dinner table?

Children know exactly how to push buttons. They screw up their little faces and declare, 'Yuck', 'That's disgusting', or 'I'm not eating that'. Meal after meal, their disapproval wears you down, leaving you exhausted. It's hard not to feel angry and perhaps a little bitter. One mother told me that when she couldn't cope anymore, she shouted, 'What's the point of me cooking at all if you're not even going to touch it?'

Anger often builds over time, after months or even years of feeding struggles. Your child's refusals can feel illogical and deeply unsettling. Why are they rejecting pasta Bolognese today when they loved it last week?

When anger takes over, we become as reactive as our children. Afterwards, guilt or shame often creeps in for not having managed the moment differently.

On a scale of 0 to 10, how intense does your anger feel at mealtimes?

Guilt and shame

Do you feel guilty after mealtimes? Ashamed of pressuring your child to eat? Worried about judgement from family and friends? Guilt is common among parents, especially when feeding doesn't go as planned.

And what about when you must explain your child's eating habits to others? Do you fear being judged or criticised for your parenting? Do you feel embarrassed when your child refuses foods their peers eat with ease? Our deep desire to nurture can easily turn into self-blame.

Eating in social situations, such as family gatherings or restaurants, can be particularly challenging. You may feel pressure to hide or downplay your child's fussy eating, intensifying feelings of shame and making it harder to seek support or advice. Perhaps you sometimes refer to your child as a fussy eater in front of others, unintentionally passing some of the embarrassment onto them.

Guilt and shame often stem from the pressure to be a perfect parent. They speak in 'shoulds': 'I should cook more. I shouldn't get frustrated. I shouldn't have pressured them last time.'

When these thoughts spiral, they can deepen feelings of failure and hopelessness.

On a scale of 0 to 10, how strongly do you experience guilt and shame in your feeding routine?

The emotional cycle of fussy eating

Graphic: The cycle of the picky eater at home (Ramos-Paul & Cardona, 2010), reproduced with permission from Luis Cardona and Barbara Marriage

Can you relate to the never-ending loop shown in the graphic above?

Your child doesn't eat, you worry, you try harder, they resist, and frustration builds–until mealtimes feel more like battles than moments of connection. Before you know it you're in a prolonged food war with no peace for anyone.

When feeding becomes this stressful, the emotional toll runs deep. Parents often describe feeling anxious before meals, tense during them, and defeated afterward. Children, too, sense the tension and may respond with avoidance, defiance, or distress–reinforcing the same pattern.

This cycle isn't just about food; it's about emotion. It can blur the boundary between caring for your child and trying to control their eating. Over time, worry can turn into guilt or even self-doubt, leaving you drained and unsure how to break free.

This cycle sheds light on why mealtimes can feel so hard. When pressure and emotion feed into each other, it's easier to understand why the pattern can feel so difficult to break.

COMMON WAYS PARENTS ADAPT UNDER FEEDING PRESSURE

When feeding feels emotionally demanding for long periods, parents naturally adapt. These adaptations aren't conscious strategies or parenting choices made lightly–they're ways of coping when pressure builds and energy runs low. They're common, human responses to a situation that feels hard to hold, day after day.

Struggling to cope

Are life's stressors affecting your ability to cope? For some parents, even organising meals or grocery shopping can start to feel over-whelming, especially when feeding difficulties stretch on over time.

Parents with support may fare better, but for others, the weight of these responsibilities can feel relentless.

Does organising meals or grocery shopping ever feel like a huge task? Perhaps you find yourself putting it off, dreading it, or feeling stuck about what to serve.

When feeding difficulties stretch on, it's often not just mealtimes that feel hard. Other life stressors can start to pile up too, making it even harder to cope day to day.

Parents with strong support may feel more buffered, but for others the weight of these combined demands can feel relentless.

Heidi is a full-time mum to three children, including one with special needs. She now also home-schools her children. Heidi does not receive extra help, and although her partner is usually around at dinner, she carries most of the feeding load.

While Heidi's situation is demanding, many parents experience a similar sense of pressure in quieter ways–through work demands, mental load, or simply being the one who always plans, shops, cooks, and worries about food.

Disengagement or giving up

Have you reached a point where it feels like you've tried everything? After repeated refusals, some parents begin serving only the foods they know will be accepted, simply to reduce stress and avoid conflict.

This response is understandable. It's a way of coping when energy is low and mealtimes feel too hard to keep pushing against.

> Louisa says she hates sitting with her children at dinner. Their complaints drive her round the bend. These days, she doesn't even try to offer something different–why bother? Instead, she simply asks her children what they want for dinner. Even then, it's not always smooth sailing, especially when they start bickering among themselves over their choices.

Overdoing it

Some parents find themselves constantly managing food concerns–preparing separate meals, keeping the kitchen open for sudden hunger, and feeling as though they're walking on eggshells at mealtimes.

Perhaps you've read about the importance of making mealtimes fun and playful, yet it feels like you're constantly putting on a performance. You try to keep the mood light with comments like,

'Daddy is eating his carrot so he can see in the dark' or 'Isn't this pasta delicious? It's so yummy!'

You might spend long stretches encouraging your child to engage with the food: 'Why don't you have a smell?' … 'Okay, now let's have a lick.'

Is this how you imagined family dinners? Do you sometimes feel more like a cheerleader, a circus clown, or a feeding therapist than a parent?

Families with fussy eaters are more likely to:

- feel responsible for their child's behaviour
- define their child by how they eat [5]
- talk more about food at meals
- end meals in arguments[6]

This is exhausting, and I imagine it's taking a toll on you.

Jake is a great home cook, but a year ago, he started making three different meals a day after one dinner ended in a massive meltdown from the twins and their older sister, Bella. The other day, the twins refused their usual go-to meal and, to avoid drama, Jake rushed back to the kitchen to make a quick bowl of pasta. As he realised he had spent most of his evening cooking separate meals to keep everyone happy, he wondered if he and his children would ever sit down and share the same meal as a family.

Confusion and self-doubt

Do you ever feel pulled in different directions about how to feed your child? Advice comes from many places–family, friends, professionals, and everyday conversations–and it doesn't always line up.

Many parents then turn to the internet hoping for clarity, but instead encounter an endless stream of tips, opinions, and quick fixes, rarely a clear or coherent plan.

Over time, this constant noise can quietly erode confidence in your own judgement, making it harder to know what to do next.

Stella tried a range of approaches–cooking recommended recipes, asking her children what they would like, and following advice from those around her. She even tried, once, sending them to bed without dinner. None of it brought lasting change.

Parental disempowerment

Amid mealtime struggles and heightened emotions, do you ever feel powerless? Conflicting advice from every direction, judgement lurking around every corner, and differences in parenting approaches–even within your own family–can all deepen this sense of disempowerment.

When parents feel overruled, unheard, or constantly second-guessed, it becomes harder to feel competent or in charge. Over time, this can quietly undermine confidence and leave you questioning yourself, even when you are doing your very best.

Lily lives with her husband, two children, and her parents. In this setup, her mother takes the lead on meal preparation and decides how she offers food to her grandchildren. Although Lily disagrees with some of her mother's strategies for managing the children's fussy eating, she feels she has little say in the matter. To make things harder, Lily's husband often sides with his mother-in-law. Meaningful discussions on the topic seem impossible. With all these factors combined, Lily feels disempowered as a parent.

Co-regulation with your child

All the pressures, emotions, and adaptations described in this chapter tend to show up most clearly here, at the table. It's amazing how quickly mealtimes can spiral. One food refusal, your patience thinning just a little, and before you know it the emotional temperature in the room has gone up several degrees. That's co-regulation under strain.

Moods are contagious. You smile and others smile back; you sigh and the room feels heavier. The same thing happens at the dinner table. Your child refuses to eat. Tension rises in you–frustration, urgency, expectation–and your child picks up on it immediately. Their body responds in kind.

This isn't your imagination, and it isn't poor parenting. It's two nervous systems having a quiet conversation through facial expression, tone of voice, and body posture. That process is called co-regulation.

When feeding has been stressful for a long time, all the adaptations you've just read about–coping, overdoing it, disengaging, doubting yourself–can make that nervous-system conversation harder to keep calm. Not because anyone is doing anything wrong, but because everyone is under pressure.

WHY HOW YOU FEEL MATTERS

Co-regulation starts with you. You've probably heard the advice given on aeroplanes: in the event of depressurisation, fit your own oxygen mask before assisting others. The same applies here.

This idea is grounded in decades of neuroscience, including the work of Stephen Porges, whose research shows that our nervous systems are constantly scanning for safety or threat–and that children rely on the adults around them to help regulate that sense of safety.

The good news is that this doesn't require overthinking. It starts with feeling sensations in your body–perhaps a knot in your stomach while cooking dinner, or a tightening in your chest just before sitting down to eat–and responding with simple grounding techniques such as bilateral movement.

One example is the butterfly hug, a self-soothing technique where you tap alternately on opposite arms. This stimulates both brain hemispheres, helping calm the nervous system and support emotional regulation during stress, anxiety, or overwhelm.

The encouraging part is this: the nervous system is changeable. Thanks to neuroplasticity–the brain's ability to form new patterns–calm responses can be learned, strengthened, and gradually become more automatic over time.

You don't need to stay calm all the time. What matters is your ability to return to calm. When you feel steadier, your child has a much better chance of feeling safe too.

A personal note

I really encourage you to work with your own internal signals–to notice how emotions show up in your body and practise gently settling them.

For many of the parents I work with, understanding their nervous system is a turning point. Once they realise their reactions are biological–not something they can simply think their way out of–everything starts to make more sense.

Calming down isn't about telling yourself to calm down or reasoning with your feelings. It begins in the body. When you soothe your body first, thoughts and emotions tend to follow.

If you're curious, take a few minutes to explore simple bilateral movement or nervous-system regulation techniques online. These body-based practices can help shift you from tension to calm–often more effectively than words alone. Just knowing your body can return to safety can change how you show up at the table.

QUICK REFLECTION

Now that you've explored the different pressures, emotions, and reactions that shape mealtimes, take a few moments to reflect. Noticing what's happening for you and how it affects your child helps you respond with more calm and confidence.

You might like to think about:

- What pressures around food or parenting feel strongest for you right now?
- Which emotions show up most often at mealtimes?
- How do they influence your tone, energy, or body language?
- Do you notice patterns–moments when emotions build or spill over?

- How do these feelings affect your ability to co-regulate with your child?
- Do you and your partner (or co-parent) share similar approaches at the table, or do they differ?
- What kind of support–family, practical, or professional– might help lighten the load?

Each small insight is a step toward calmer, more connected meals.

CHAPTER 4

PEACE OF MIND SOLUTIONS

Before you can create the calm, supportive environment your child needs to overcome fussy eating, you need reassurance that their nutrition is taken care of. When you have peace of mind about this, everything else becomes easier.

This chapter focuses on easing nutritional worry, not as a cure in itself, but as a way to settle the background anxiety that can otherwise undermine calm and co-regulation.

It offers practical ways to support your child's nutritional needs, helping you feel more confident, grounded, and ready to focus on connection rather than worry.

NUTRITIONAL DEFICIENCIES

Most typical fussy eaters do fine with nutrition. However, some studies report lower iron and zinc in fussy-eating children. If your child is missing entire food groups and you suspect they are at risk of nutritional deficiencies, consult with a doctor.[1]

Assessing your child's nutritional status is straightforward. Doctors can order blood tests to assess the nutritional status for iron, zinc, vitamin D, vitamin B12, folate (B9), selenium and calcium. Dietitians and nutri-

31

tionists can estimate nutritional intake through accurate food diaries, typically based on a three-to-five-day recall of your child's intake of food.

SUPPLEMENTING AND TWEAKING FOOD

Consider your child's nutritional needs by distinguishing between optimising their intake of vitamins and minerals and/or simply increasing their calorie consumption.

Multivitamins and mineral supplements

All-in-one multivitamins and mineral supplements are widely available over the counter. Most are formulated to meet basic micronutrient needs and are generally safe to use without a prescription. Alongside other nutrients, they typically contain between 2.5 and 5 mg of iron, varying amounts of zinc, and a range of essential vitamins.

Knowing your child is getting the micronutrients they need can offer peace of mind, especially if you have lingering concerns. If you're unsure, speak to your pharmacist.

If your child lacks calcium in their diet, consult your doctor or dietitian about whether a supplement is appropriate.

I don't recommend giving high doses of iron–or any single micronutrient–without professional guidance. When individual micronutrients are given separately rather than as part of a formulation, they may compete for absorption in the body. For example, calcium, zinc, and iron can interfere with one another's uptake if not dosed correctly or spaced apart. This is why professional advice is essential when considering separate or high-dose supplementation.

Doctors can prescribe targeted supplements based on blood tests that confirm a deficiency.

Fortified foods

Fortified foods, such as iron-fortified breakfast cereals and bread, can be an easy and palatable way to boost iron intake. Designed to deliver specific nutrients, fortified foods help bridge the gap between your child's nutritional needs and what they may be missing due to limited food choices. These include breakfast cereals, milk or plant-based milk, bread, and fortified fruit juices or sports drinks.

Nutritional supplements

Doctors or dietitians may sometimes recommend nutritional supplements–usually in liquid or powdered form–that provide essential vitamins, minerals, and macronutrients such as fats, carbohydrates, and protein.

I don't recommend self-prescribing these products, as some children may start eating even fewer solid foods and become reliant on a liquid diet. When used under professional guidance, however, supplements can play a helpful role for children who struggle to meet their nutritional needs.

Calorie concerns and enriched foods

Some children with autism, ADHD, or severe anxiety may eat only small amounts before losing interest. Providing high-calorie foods in small portions can help.

Adding oils such as olive oil, avocado oil, coconut oil, cream, or butter to dishes can significantly increase their calorific content.

You can also include:

- **Fats and oils**: Butter, olive oil, and other plant oils can be added to vegetables, pasta, rice, mashed potato, soups, and sauces to increase energy intake without increasing portion size.
- **Nuts, seeds, and nut butters**: Peanut butter, almond butter, and other nut butters are calorie-dense and can be spread on toast, added to smoothies, or used as a dip.
- **Avocado**: Rich in healthy fats and adds a creamy texture to sandwiches, salads, and wraps.

- **Full-fat dairy**: Whole milk, full-fat yoghurt, and regular cheese are energy dense options. Milk powder can be mixed into yoghurt, smoothies, quiches, or pancake to increase calories, protein, and calcium without changing taste or texture too much.
- **Dried fruit**: Raisins, dates, apricots, and other dried fruits are concentrated sources of calories and can be added to cereal, yoghurt, and baked goods.
- **Coconut products**: Coconut flakes, shredded coconut, and coconut cream can enhance the energy content of both sweet and savoury dishes.
- **Natural sweeteners**: Honey, maple syrup, and agave nectar can be drizzled over foods to increase calorie intake.
- **Condiments**: Creamy dressings, sauces, mayonnaise, and spreads can boost the caloric value of meals.
- **Meat and poultry**: Ham and turkey can be included in sandwiches, salads, and main dishes, or blended into soups or sauces to create a smooth texture.

YOUR CHILD'S IMMUNE SYSTEM, ANXIETY LEVELS, AND OVERALL HEALTH

Researchers are exploring the intricate links between the brain, immune system, and gut flora, also known as the microbiota of the gastrointestinal system. The bacteria present in a child's gut from birth onwards play a vital role in developing and training the immune system.[2]

Essentially, the immune system 'learns' from these microbial inhabitants, forming a symbiotic relationship that influences a child's health over time.

A balanced gut microbiota supports overall health, whereas imbalances–known as dysbiosis–have been associated to a range of conditions, including inflammatory bowel disease, obesity, allergies, type 2 diabetes, autism, and even colorectal cancer.[3]

Maintaining a healthy balance of 'good bacteria' may have a significant impact on both daily and long-term wellbeing.

Some studies have also explored the connection between gut flora and anxiety. Dietary adjustments that influence gut bacteria–such as consuming prebiotic fibre and live cultures–may play a role in managing anxiety. In fact, a review published in the British Medical Journal found that more than half (52%) of the 21 studies examining gut microbiota regulation reported a positive impact on anxiety symptoms. [4]

Nutrition plays a pivotal role in cultivating a healthy gut microbiota. There are three key ways to nourish and replenish the gut flora throughout life: probiotics, fermented foods and prebiotics.

Probiotics

Probiotics are live microorganisms that, when consumed in sufficient amounts, provide health benefits. The term 'probiotic' is used only for microbes with scientifically documented advantages.[5]Over-the-counter probiotic supplements are widely available and generally safe for daily use, except for those who are immunocompromised. They may also be beneficial after a course of antibiotics.

Fermented foods

For thousands of years, humans have used fermented foods as a source of beneficial bacteria, similar to probiotics. These foods naturally contain live cultures that support gut health. Examples include yoghurt, kefir, fresh kimchi, sauerkraut, water or brine-cured olives, traditional salami, and certain cheeses. However, pasteurised, heated, or cooked fermented foods–such as tempeh, soy sauce, sourdough bread, and chocolate–no longer contain live cultures.

Prebiotics

Prebiotics are types of fibre that feed beneficial gut bacteria–without them, these bacteria cannot survive or thrive. Monash University identifies several everyday foods that contain prebiotic fibres. The list below is not exhaustive.

- **Vegetables**: Garlic, onions, leeks, spring onions, asparagus, Jerusalem artichokes
- **Fruits**: Bananas (especially slightly green), watermelon
- **Legumes**: Chickpeas, lentils, kidney beans
- **Grains**: Barley, oats, whole wheat
- **Nuts and seeds**: Cashews, pistachios

Prebiotic supplements are also available over the counter.

Synbiotics

Synbiotics refer to a combination of probiotics and prebiotics that work synergistically to promote a healthy balance of microorganisms in the gut. They can be bought over the counter too.

QUICK REFLECTION

Now that you've read this chapter, you can decide how best to support your child's nutrition.

Consider the following questions:

- Do you need to consult a professional about your child's nutritional intake or growth?
- Would a giving your child a vitamin and mineral supplement provide you with peace of mind?
- Are there gaps in your child's eating that are causing you ongoing worry?

With a clearer understanding of your child's nutritional needs and how to address them, you can move forward with confidence and peace of mind.

CHAPTER 5
DIAGNOSTICS AND FEEDING THERAPY

Not every child with feeding challenges will receive a formal diagnosis–but those with more complex needs often will. In these cases, conditions such as *Paediatric Feeding Disorder (PFD)* or *Avoidant/Restrictive Food Intake Disorder (ARFID)* may be identified.

This chapter is not about labelling your child or rushing into therapy. It's here to help you understand when feeding difficulties may benefit from professional input, what different pathways mean, and how to make informed decisions without panic.

It will help you to:

- gain a broad understanding of PFD and ARFID so you can discuss them confidently with your doctor or healthcare provider
- learn what kinds of feeding therapies and multidisciplinary services are available
- explore how hypnotherapy can complement traditional approaches by addressing emotional and sensory aspects of eating

By understanding both the diagnostic and therapeutic landscape, you can make informed choices about the next steps for your child–whether that means seeking an assessment, accessing specialist therapy, or finding supportive strategies at home.

ARFID AND PFD

Avoidant/Restrictive Food Intake Disorder (ARFID) and *Paediatric Feeding Disorder (PFD)* are two conditions that involve significant difficulties with eating and feeding. Although they may seem similar, they are distinct conditions with different causes and treatment approaches. [1]

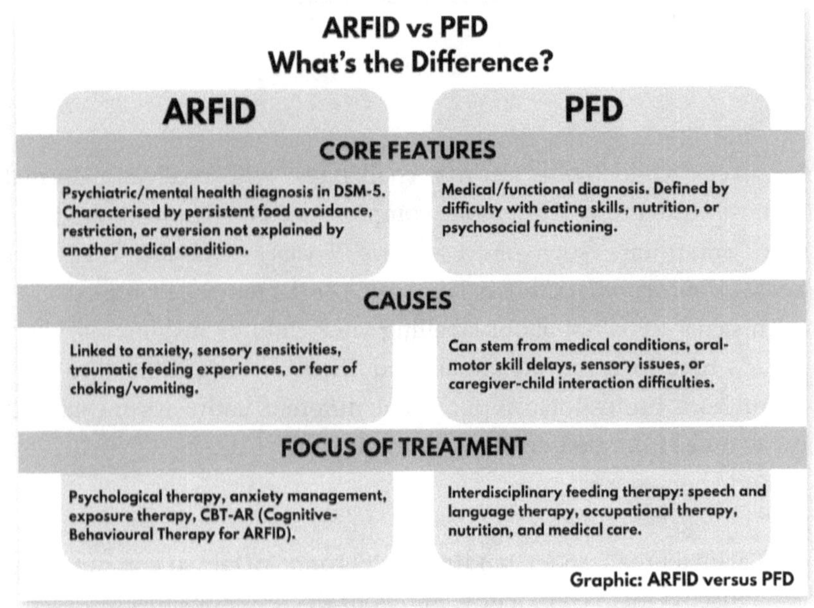

Children with ARFID often avoid food because of sensory sensitivities, fear of choking or vomiting, or other distressing past experiences with eating. Some simply have very little interest in eating, which can lead to poor growth or nutrition.

Children with PFD tend to have physical or functional feeding difficulties. These may involve trouble chewing or swallowing safely, delayed oral-motor skills, or challenges managing certain textures or consistencies.

Getting a diagnosis

A diagnosis of ARFID or PFD can be helpful for families struggling with severe feeding difficulties.

- **ARFID**: Assessment usually involves a multidisciplinary team. A psychiatrist, psychologist, or paediatrician may confirm the diagnosis, while dietitians and other health professionals often support assessment and treatment.
- **PFD**: Assessment is typically led by a medical practitioner, who may coordinate input from specialists such as dietitians, occupational therapists (OTs), and speech and language pathologists (SLPs).

Some parents may feel more comfortable with a medical diagnosis such as PFD, while others may prefer the clarity of ARFID, which is classified as a mental health diagnosis. In some cases, children may not meet the full criteria for either diagnosis, despite ongoing difficulties. Sometimes, there is overlap between conditions, and different professionals may diagnose based on their scope of practice.

Receiving a diagnosis can bring clarity and reassurance–but it's not a cure. Progress still takes time, and your role as a parent remains central. The approaches outlined in this book are designed to work alongside professional therapies, or to help families who have completed feeding therapy and still need additional support at home.

FEEDING THERAPY

Feeding therapy is usually provided by a multidisciplinary team–speech and language pathologists, occupational therapists, dietitians, and psychologists–each bringing a different lens to support eating and feeding.

Over time, the field has evolved. Early approaches often focused on behaviour–prompting, rewarding, or encouraging children to eat. While these methods were well-intentioned, they could create pressure, leaving children anxious and parents exhausted.

Today, feeding therapy looks very different. It's more sensory-aware, relationship-based, and family-centred. Therapists now focus less on getting food into a child's mouth and more on helping them feel relaxed, safe, and in control around food.

Responsive feeding therapy, which I align with in my own practice, focuses on coaching parents first. Rather than directing the child's eating, therapists guide parents to change the mealtime dynamic itself–how food is offered, how communication unfolds, and how emotional safety is maintained. Parents learn to tune into both their own reactions and their child's cues, creating the foundation for calm co-regulation.

Hypnotherapy for feeding issues

Children who struggle with extreme fussy eating often experience repeated fight, flight, or freeze responses at mealtimes. Avoidance brings short-term relief but reinforces a negative 'fussy eater' identity, making change even harder.

A Journey of Extreme Fussy Eating

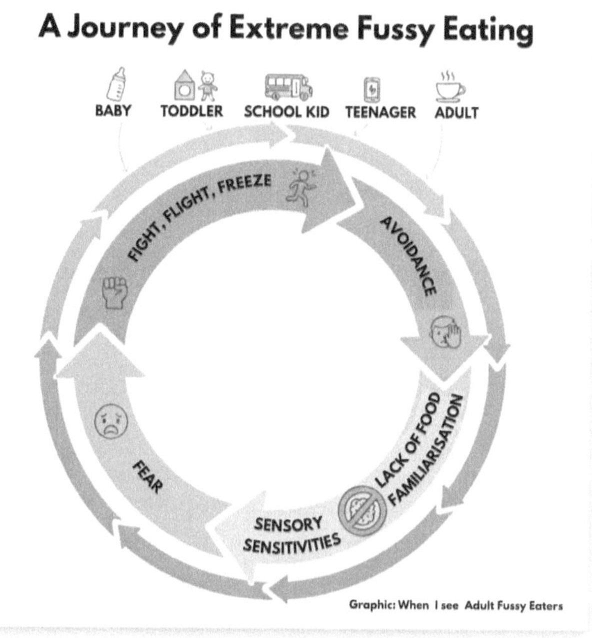

Graphic: When I see Adult Fussy Eaters

A supportive mealtime environment, grounded in responsive feeding principles, is the essential first step. Once that foundation is in place, hypnotherapy can be a powerful complement. Gentle, age-appropriate sessions guide children into deep relaxation, interrupting the automatic stress responses that food can trigger. In this calmer state, they can begin to reframe their reactions, reduce anxiety, and feel more confident about exploring and accepting new foods.

Hypnotherapy can also support children with more complex challenges, such as ARFID, swallowing or choking phobias, and certain gastrointestinal difficulties like *Irritable bowel syndrome* (IBS).[2]

Importantly, hypnotherapy can help interrupt the cycle that carries fussy eating into adulthood. When fight, flight, or freeze responses repeatedly drive avoidance and food exploration remains limited, sensitivities persist. By breaking out of this loop early, children can avoid growing into adults who continue to struggle with food anxiety, limited diets, or sensory-driven avoidance.

QUICK REFLECTION

Now that you've finished this chapter, you may have a clearer sense of whether additional support would be helpful and whether a diagnosis could provide valuable insight into your child's fussy eating.

Consider these questions as you reflect on your next steps:

- Would having a medical or mental health diagnosis help your family better understand your child's feeding challenges?
- Who could walk alongside your family as you take the next steps toward easier mealtimes?

If you decide to seek professional support, speaking with your doctor about a referral to a paediatrician is a good first step. Since wait-lists for paediatricians can be long, it may be helpful to book an appointment now, even as you begin working through the Reboots in Section 5. And if, in the meantime, you realise you no longer need the appointment—what a win!—you can always cancel it later.

SECTION 2: CUT YOUR CHILD SOME SLACK

In this section, we'll explore what distinguishes a typical fussy eater from an extreme fussy eater. You'll be introduced to seven continua that highlight different aspects of feeding challenges, helping you reflect on where your child might sit along each one.

The goal is to better understand your child's unique experience, so you can meet them with empathy and create an environment where progress feels possible.

ABOUT THE CONTINUA

The seven continua are not standardised tests but rather tools for observation. Think of it as gathering insights–like adding possible reasons for your child's eating difficulties into a shopping basket. The more you add, the heavier it feels. The aim is to understand what's in the basket, so over time, you can lighten the load.

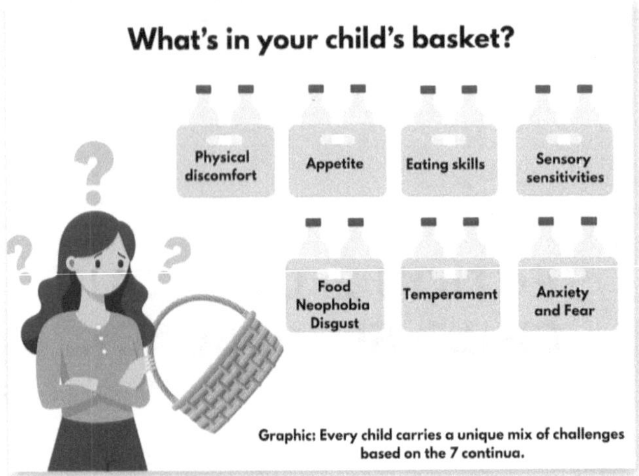

Graphic: Every child carries a unique mix of challenges based on the 7 continua.

The seven continua are:

- **Physical discomfort**: Are any medical or physical concerns making eating uncomfortable or difficult?
- **Appetite**: Does your child show natural signs of hunger, or do they often seem uninterested in food?
- **Eating skills**: Is your child developing age-appropriate chewing, swallowing, and food-handling skills? Are they still learning how flavours and textures work?
- **Sensory sensitivities**: Do texture, smell, temperature, or taste strongly influence your child's willingness to eat?
- **Food neophobia & disgust**: How intense is your child's resistance to new, mixed, or visually unfamiliar foods?
- **Temperament**: Is your child naturally cautious, strong-willed, or slow to warm up?
- **Anxiety & fear**: Are worries about choking, vomiting, or past negative experiences affecting eating? Does your child show fight, flight, or freeze responses around food?

Typical fussy eaters

If your child sits toward the lower end (left side) of the continua over-all, they likely fall within the typical fussy-eater range. With the right environment and gentle support, progress often comes more easily and steadily.

Extreme fussy eaters

If your child tends to fall further along each continuum, they may align more closely with the *extreme fussy eater* profile. In these cases, extra guidance or professional assessment can be helpful. Still, the most important factor remains creating a calm, supportive environment that builds your child's confidence around food.

In the next seven chapters, we'll look at each continuum in more detail. You don't need to absorb everything at once–think of this section as a map. You can zoom in on areas that feel most relevant, or simply step back to see the bigger picture. If anything you read raises concerns, these insights can help you have more informed conversations with your doctor.

CHAPTER 6

CONTINUUM 1–PHYSICAL DISCOMFORT AND GENERAL HEALTH

Sometimes, a child's reluctance to eat isn't about behaviour at all–it's about how their body feels.

Pain, reflux, congestion, or other medical issues can quietly create negative associations with food. When eating feels unpleasant–or when it has unpleasant consequences–the body reacts automatically, tightening up, pulling away, or shutting down. These are instinctive fight, flight, or freeze responses designed to protect us from danger.

If eating has ever caused discomfort, it's understandable that your child might start avoiding food altogether. Over time, what began as a physical reaction can turn into an emotional one, as the body learns to associate eating with stress or unease.

For some families, the connection between health and feeding is clear. Their child has faced medical challenges, hospital stays, or treatments that understandably disrupted eating. For others, there may be no obvious medical history, yet discomfort still plays a hidden role.

This section invites you to pause and notice the adjustments you may have made to help your child eat more comfortably. Many parents adapt instinctively: removing foods that seem to cause trouble, relying on distractions such as screens, or feeding babies while they are sleepy–dream feeds–to avoid distress.

These accommodations are understandable and often effective in the short term. They help meals get done. But sometimes, they also quietly mask an underlying problem. When eating only feels possible with distraction, reduced awareness, or avoidance, it can be a sign that discomfort is still present.

Looking back at how your child eats–when it feels easier and when it doesn't–can offer important clues. These patterns don't point to parenting mistakes; they point to a body that may be trying to protect itself.

In this chapter, we'll look at two key areas of physical discomfort that can affect eating:

1. **The gastrointestinal tract**: conditions such as reflux, allergies, intolerances, constipation, and abdominal pain.
2. **The upper airways**: issues like chronic congestion, enlarged tonsils or adenoids, and mouth breathing, all of which can make eating physically harder or less pleasant.

A note on seeking professional guidance

As you read on, you'll see references to seeking professional support. This doesn't mean something is 'wrong' or that every child needs treatment. It simply reflects that suspected physical discomfort is best assessed with guidance.

Unless there is a known anaphylactic allergy, it's best not to remove foods from your child's diet before medical assessment, as this can complicate diagnosis and testing. Your healthcare provider can guide you on safe next steps.

PART 1: THE GASTROINTESTINAL TRACT– WHEN EATING HURTS INSIDE

Discomfort in the gastrointestinal tract can take many forms–heartburn, bloating, constipation, nausea, vomiting, or tummy pain. When eating causes discomfort, it's easy to see why food might become something to avoid.

Reflux and GORD

Reflux occurs when stomach contents flow back into the oesophagus, causing discomfort. In some cases, babies and children are prescribed medication for gastro-oesophageal reflux disease (GORD), a more persistent and severe form of reflux.

GORD is relatively common in both infants and children. In infants, it affects around 50% of babies under three months, with most cases resolving by their first birthday.[1] Among older children, prevalence ranges from 2–8%, depending on age and population.[2]

In babies, signs may include:

- frequent spitting up or vomiting (especially after feeds)
- refusing to eat unless sleepy or distracted
- crying or irritability during or after feeding, sometimes with back arching
- poor weight gain or weight loss
- discomfort when lying flat, such as unsettled sleep, frequent waking, or distress when placed on their back

In children, signs may include:

- recurrent vomiting or regurgitation after meals
- coughing (especially at night or when lying down)
- wheezing or choking
- refusing food or eating only small amounts
- refusing to eat unless distracted, prompted
- preferring soft, smooth, or blended foods and avoiding textures that require more chewing or swallowing effort
- frequent swallowing, throat clearing, or lip smacking, sometimes used unconsciously to soothe a burning or uncomfortable sensation in the throat
- complaining of heartburn or chest discomfort[3]
- discomfort when lying flat after meals, which may show up as restlessness, bedtime resistance, or difficulty settling to sleep

Seeking medical guidance at this stage can relieve both the symptoms and the stress that quietly reinforces feeding difficulties.

Allergies

If your child has a diagnosed food allergy, you may have noticed their fussy eating started or worsened after the diagnosis. This is common. [4] Many children develop a fear of eating new foods or foods they are unsure about, worrying they might contain the allergen and cause a reaction. Over time, this can lead to a limited diet and a reliance on familiar 'safe' foods.

Some allergies go undiagnosed for a while, leading to discomfort such as reflux, abdominal pain, or bloating, which may be misunderstood. Children with a family history of allergies, asthma, eczema, or hay fever are at higher risk of developing food allergies. [5]

The most common allergenic foods in children include dairy, eggs, peanuts, tree nuts, soy, wheat, fish, and shellfish.

One condition worth knowing about is *Eosinophilic Oesophagitis (EoE)*–an allergic inflammation of the oesophagus that can cause pain, difficulty swallowing, or food getting stuck. Though rare, EoE can make eating uncomfortable and may explain why some children seem fearful of food.

Whatever the cause, identifying allergies or EoE helps relieve discomfort and supports safer, more comfortable eating, without unnecessary restriction.

Intolerances and coeliac disease

Food intolerances can make eating uncomfortable, but unlike allergies, they don't involve the immune system. Instead, they stem from difficulty digesting certain foods, often leading to bloating, gas, nausea, or abdominal pain. Over time, children may begin avoiding foods they associate with these sensations.

Lactose intolerance is one of the most common examples. It occurs when the body lacks the enzyme needed to digest lactose, the natural sugar in milk. Other sensitivities can involve gluten, fructose, histamine, or certain food additives.

Coeliac disease is sometimes mistaken for an intolerance, but it is an autoimmune condition in which gluten damages the lining of the small intestine. Symptoms can be subtle, variable, or delayed, and some children remain undiagnosed for years. Awareness and timely investigation by a GP who is alert to coeliac disease can make a significant difference to how quickly families receive clarity and support.

Because testing relies on an active immune response, coeliac disease can only be accurately assessed while gluten is still part of the diet. This is why professional guidance is essential when symptoms raise concern.

Vomiting

Vomiting can occur for many reasons–from reflux, intolerances or a temporary stomach bug. But whatever the cause, it's an intensely sensory experience: the nausea, the taste, the smell, and the physical strain can make it deeply unpleasant. The oesophagus may become irritated, and for sensitive or anxious children, the memory of that discomfort can linger long after the illness has passed. The child's brain is simply trying to prevent another unpleasant experience. [6]

Constipation

Many children experience constipation. The Royal Children's Hospital in Melbourne notes it affects up to 30% of children at some point.

When passing stools is painful or uncomfortable, children may begin to associate toileting with distress. This fear, known as *faecal anxiety*, can lead children to hold in stools, worsening the problem and causing emotional distress. Chronic constipation may lead to faecal impaction, sudden incontinence, or abdominal pain.

In most cases, medical treatment helps relieve discomfort and break this cycle. Addressing constipation can make children feel lighter, more comfortable, and more willing to eat.

> Six-year-old Oliver suffers from chronic constipation. Most recently, he had to be hospitalised due to faecal impaction. His parents report that he often gets anxious at mealtimes and refuses to eat food that could, in principle, help with his constipation. Oliver now takes a laxative every day, as prescribed by his doctor.

Bloating, abdominal pain, gas and cramping, diarrhoea

Persistent bloating, tummy pain, gas, cramping, or diarrhoea can understandably reduce appetite and disrupt eating. These symptoms should be assessed by a doctor to rule out medical causes such as allergies, intolerances, coeliac disease, or IBS.

Sometimes, however, no clear medical cause is found.[7] This is known as *Functional Abdominal Pain (FAP)*–where the gut is healthy, but the discomfort is real. For some children, the pain is constant; for others it comes and goes.

Psychosocial factors–stress, anxiety, or heightened interoception–increased awareness of internal sensations–can amplify these symptoms and make eating feel unpredictable or unsafe. Children with autism spectrum disorder (ASD) are also more likely to experience bloating, constipation, diarrhoea, or irregular stool patterns that affect feeding.

You'll see this idea again later in the Sensory section, where we explore how children interpret internal sensations, and how interoception can make normal digestive feelings seem painful or alarming.

Recognising these symptoms early helps guide appropriate support and intervention, particularly when feeding difficulties begin to affect dietary variety, nutritional intake, or eating patterns over time.[8]

PART 2: THE UPPER AIRWAYS–WHEN BREATHING AFFECTS EATING

Breathing and eating share the same space the mouth and throat.

When airflow or swallowing is disrupted, eating can become physically harder, less enjoyable, or even anxiety-provoking.

Mouth-breathing, congestion, tonsils, adenoids and dentition

Some children breathe through their mouths due to congestion, allergies, or enlarged tonsils and adenoids. Mouth-breathing can dry the mouth, dull taste and smell, and make food seem bland or unpleasant, similar to what you feel when you have a cold. It also alters jaw and tongue position, affecting how children chew, swallow and learn to eat. [9], [10] Orthodontics and orofacial functional myotherapy may be useful to reduce mouth-breathing[11] and tongue-thrust.[12]

Enlarged tonsils can make swallowing effortful, catch food, and increase choking risk. Enlarged adenoids sit behind the nasal cavity, and when swollen, they can block nasal airflow, creating a constant 'stuffy' feeling. This dependence on mouth-breathing further disrupts normal swallowing and chewing patterns. Some children develop a muffled or 'hot-potato' voice and may prefer soft foods or take longer to chew. In more significant cases, chronic mouth-breathing can contribute to snoring, sleep apnoea, night-time drooling, agitated sleep, and daytime irritability.[13], [14] Mouth breathers are more likely to have ADHD than nasal breathers.[15]

Children who tire easily–due to health challenges or airway discomfort–may eat slowly, avoid certain textures, or prefer soft foods that require less effort.

> Three-year-old Emma shows little appetite and a strong preference for sweetened food concerns her mother. Emma's health history includes viral wheeze, inflamed and enlarged adenoids, resulting in several hospital stays over the last three years. She still mouth-breathes and is under the care of an ENT. She always wants to sweeten her morning oats and generously uses ketchup on various foods. As we ponder on her small appetite parents realise Emma will do better if they let her

enhance the taste of food, within good measure, with taste she can detect.

Dysphagia and swallowing difficulties

Swallowing problems can occur when the muscles and reflexes of the mouth and throat are poorly coordinated or weakened–often following respiratory illness, early intubation, or neurological conditions. *Dysphagia,* the medical term for difficulty swallowing, can cause pain, the sensation of food 'sticking' in the throat, or coughing and gagging during meals. Even mild discomfort can make a child cautious about eating, especially if past experiences were distressing. Speech pathologists specialising in feeding can assess swallowing safety and guide exercises to improve strength, timing, and confidence.

 Charlotte was born ten weeks premature and required tube feeding until discharge. At around six months old, she struggled with the introduction of solid foods and remained reliant on purées, gradually losing interest in eating. Observing her swallowing difficulties, her parents wondered whether eating was uncomfortable for her.

A speech pathologist assessed Charlotte and identified signs of dysphagia, possibly related to early medical interventions such as intubation. With therapy, Charlotte gradually learned to eat more comfortably, and as her tissues healed and coordination improved, her feeding skills developed.

Dentition and oral comfort

Dental pain, misalignment, or delayed tooth eruption can affect a child's willingness to bite and chew. Malocclusion, missing teeth, or sensory sensitivity in the mouth can make food feel uncomfortable or unpredictable. For some children, dental treatment or orthodontic care can markedly improve feeding comfort.

Twelve-year-old Alex has a lower-jaw overbite, which keeps his mouth slightly open and makes it difficult for him to fully close his lips, often leading to drooling. Because he cannot cut food with his front teeth, he relies solely on his molars to chew, making eating an exhausting task. When asked about the challenge, Alex simply describes it as 'exhausting'–a word that captures how much effort eating takes for him. His mother has become increasingly aware of how mouth breathing affects not just his eating, but his daily comfort.

Gagging

Gagging is a natural protective reflex that helps prevent choking. When the throat detects a potential obstruction, the body's automatic response contracts muscles to expel the object, ensuring safe swallowing.

Most babies experience gagging as they learn to eat, and this is a normal part of development. However, when gagging becomes frequent, intense, or distressing, it warrants closer attention.

One possible contributor is enlarged tonsils, which can reduce space in the throat and make swallowing more difficult. Other medical factors can also play a role, including dysphagia and gastro-oesophageal reflux disease (GORD), particularly when discomfort or irritation affects swallowing.[16]

A heightened gag reflex can also be triggered by smell or flavour, particularly in children with sensory hypersensitivities or sensory processing challenges. Gagging often worsens under pressure to eat. If this becomes a concern, it's worth seeking support from a doctor, speech and language therapist, or occupational therapist.

Frequent gagging may cause a child to avoid certain foods or textures and, in some cases, lead to a general reluctance to eat.

Seven-year-old Richard has had extensive feeding therapy over the last three years. When his speech pathologist identified a tongue-tie, it became clear that his frequent gagging was not sensory, as previously assumed, but functional. Before this was recognised, Richard had grown increasingly anxious about eating, fearing that something would go wrong. Gagging at nearly every meal was not only unpleasant but gradually led him to avoid foods that felt unsafe.

Choking incidents and traumatic incidents

Choking incidents can instil fear and anxiety in children as well as their parents, leading to food aversions and tense mealtimes for everyone. [17,18]

While incidents may happen unexpectedly, it's important to explore underlying reasons such as swallowing difficulties (dysphagia), gastro-oesophageal reflux (GORD), anxiety, or sensory hypersensitivities.

Professional help is often needed to address these issues effectively. Some anxious or obsessive-compulsive children may develop *phagophobia* (fear of swallowing/choking) even without a physical cause. [19] Cognitive-behavioural therapy, psychotherapy, or hypnotherapy can be helpful in these cases.

When illness affects taste and smell

Viral infections–such as colds, flu, or COVID-19–can temporarily alter a child's sense of taste and smell, leading to sudden pickiness, reduced appetite, or avoidance of familiar foods. Some children may find their favourite foods taste 'off,' while others struggle with a dulled sense of smell that makes meals less appealing.

Research shows that a sudden loss of smell can lead to changes in appetite, weight loss, and, in some cases, depression. [20] Smell plays a vital role in food-seeking, food preferences, and the metabolic pathways that regulate hunger and satiety. [21] For children, the sense of smell is especially important: it often precedes vision, reaching them before they even lay eyes on food, sparking curiosity and stimulating appetite.

QUICK REFLECTION

- Where would you place your child on this continuum of discomfort?
- Has eating ever been linked to pain, fear, or physical effort for your child? If so, how might those experiences still influence their appetite today?
- Have you made accommodations to help your child eat more comfortably–such as changing foods, textures, routines, or using distraction?
- Would it be helpful to discuss these observations with your doctor or a feeding specialist?

CHAPTER 7

CONTINUUM 2–APPETITE

Appetite is at the heart of eating. It motivates your child to seek food, take the first bite, and continue eating until their body feels satisfied. Without appetite, mealtimes can quickly become stressful or task-focused, and any progress with food becomes much harder to sustain.

That's why appetite deserves attention. It's a key indicator of a child's comfort, confidence, and physical wellbeing. Appetite is our ally in this journey–we need it on board, and we need to understand how well it's working for your child.

THE ABILITY OF CHILDREN TO SELF-REGULATE THEIR FOOD INTAKE

Even from birth, children have an incredible ability to tune into their own hunger and fullness signals. A breastfeeding baby, for instance, will stop drawing milk and drift to sleep when they've had enough.[1]

As babies grow, this internal wisdom continues. Research shows that infants and young preschoolers naturally adjust how much they eat depending on the energy content of their food or formula.[2] When meals are more calorie-dense, they eat less; when meals are lighter, they eat more. Their bodies instinctively balance their intake to meet their energy needs.

Toddlers, of course, bring their own rhythm. One day they eat with great enthusiasm, the next they barely touch their food. Yet, when you look at what they consume over the course of a week, it almost always adds up to exactly what their bodies require.[3] Many parents also notice that fussy toddlers tend to eat best in the morning–their bodies are simply managing energy for the day ahead.

These patterns remind us that appetite is, by nature, self-regulating. Most children are born with the ability to balance how much they eat according to their body's needs. [4] What can interfere with this ability are external influences–like medical factors, pressure to eat, anxiety, or sensory sensitivities–which can cloud those natural cues.

Enabling children to eat to satisfaction

Eating to satisfaction plays a crucial role in fostering healthy eating habits. It also can support children who otherwise under-eat. It involves tuning into the body's natural hunger and fullness signals, stopping when we feel comfortably satisfied rather than overly full.

For instance, when enjoying a slice of chocolate cake, the first bite is intensely delicious. As we continue eating, our enjoyment gradually diminishes. This natural decline in pleasure signals that we have had enough, allowing us to stop eating without feeling deprived.

Eating to satisfaction is an intuitive process. The more we trust our body's signals, and those of our children, the healthier our relationship with food becomes. When we respond to these signals, we are less likely to fixate on food between meals, as the body has received the nutrients and energy it needs to function well at mealtimes. [5] This reduces the urge to snack excessively or overeat later, fostering a more balanced relationship with food.

The goal is to create an environment where children can naturally learn to eat to satisfaction. Our Meal System is consistent with this idea.

Perception of appetite and growth charts

Worry about appetite is common. For some families, it reflects genuine concerns about growth; for others, it persists despite reassuring growth patterns.

Understanding growth patterns accurately helps you know when to seek help and when to relax. Misinterpreting growth charts can either delay important action or create unnecessary pressure.

Research consistently shows that most fussy eaters grow just as well as their peers. Their BMI, height, and weight usually follow a steady trajectory, even when their eating seems limited. [6]

Yet many parents still feel anxious about appetite, despite the growth chart telling a reassuring story. You might think, 'My baby eats more than my two-year-old,' or 'My child has always been on the fifth percentile, but he's so thin.' These reactions are common and usually stem from how growth is perceived, not from actual calorific deficiency.

Many assume the 50th percentile represents 'normal' weight. In truth, healthy growth falls anywhere between the 3rd and 97th percentiles. [7] Genetics plays a major role; some children are naturally smaller or larger, and their appetite usually aligns perfectly with their body's needs. [8]

During infancy, growth is rapid. Most babies double their birth weight by six months and triple it by one year. [9] This high demand for energy explains their frequent feeding.

Between two and five years, growth slows down. Toddlers typically gain 1–2 kilograms and grow 6–8 centimetres per year, so their appetite adjusts accordingly. [10]

Growth charts are designed to track patterns over time, not to rank children. Viewing them as a scorecard can create unnecessary anxiety or pressure to make a child eat more. What matters most is consistency–a steady curve that shows a child's needs are being met.

If you're uncertain about what your child's growth means, ask your doctor or dietitian to walk you through it. They can confirm whether growth is steady or if further assessment is needed. [11] Understanding these patterns helps you act when necessary and let go of worry when growth is on track.

FACTORS THAT INFLUENCE APPETITE

A child's appetite can fluctuate for many reasons. Beyond normal day-to-day variation, certain physiological factors–such as stress responses, medication, or nutritional deficiencies–can suppress hunger or disrupt the body's natural regulation of food intake.

Anxiety, stress responses and appetite

As you reflect on a time in your life when you felt anxious, did you notice any change in your appetite?

Many parents describe their extreme fussy eater as anxious.[12] It's understandable to want to increase how much your child eats by topping up meals or encouraging extra bites.

However, this can interfere with the body's natural ability to self-regulate food intake and often has the opposite effect. When a child feels pressured to eat, their appetite may switch off altogether. Instead of eating more, they may eat less than they would have naturally.[13] Some children even tell you they're full simply to avoid the situation, only to mention they're hungry again later once they feel calm and safe.

Medication and appetite

Medication can have a profound effect on appetite. For instance, stimulant medications used to manage ADHD often reduce daytime hunger, which can lead to skipped meals or weight loss.

With careful medical management, doctors can often keep these effects under control. Good communication is essential–any loss of appetite should be discussed early, and the doctor should regularly monitor the child's weight so there is clear data to guide decisions.

Once the doctor has a clear picture of what's happening at home, treatment can often be adjusted effectively. Too often, I see communication gaps leave parents feeling uncertain or helpless.

> Elliot is a nine-year-old diagnosed with ASD and ADHD. He takes medication, and his parents can see it is beneficial. Recently, however, Elliot's appetite has decreased to a worrying level.
>
> One evening at dinner, his father, desperate to encourage him to eat, began pleading—which ended in a meltdown. Elliot is somewhat aware of what's happening; he recently told his father, 'I'm paper-thin. I could fly in the wind.'

Elliot's paediatrician adjusted his medication, which led to a healthy weight gain of 3 kg. Not long after, Elliot exclaimed, 'Mum, can you make more? I think I'm going to eat all of it.'

Low iron and appetite

Iron deficiency can have a marked effect on appetite. The connection isn't fully understood, but research suggests that low iron disrupts the balance of hunger and satiety hormones. [14]

Leptin, the hormone that signals fullness, and ghrelin, the hormone that stimulates hunger, both depend on healthy iron metabolism. [15, 16] When iron is low, these signals can become dysregulated, reducing a child's natural drive to eat.

Iron deficiency can also influence behaviour and sensory interest in food. Some children develop pica—cravings for non-food items such as dirt, clay, or ice—while others show irritability, fatigue, or low concentration that further suppress appetite. [17] Low iron and ferritin levels, along with vitamin D deficiency, have also been linked with ADHD.[18]

Children who are extreme fussy eaters, or who follow vegetarian or vegan diets, are at higher risk of low iron intake. So are infants, toddlers, and adolescents during rapid growth phases, as well as premature or low birthweight babies whose iron stores are naturally lower. [19]

High milk intake after 12 months–more than about 500 mL per day–is associated with poorer iron status in children.[20] Because cow's milk is low in iron and its high calcium and casein content can reduce iron absorption, drinking large volumes may compete with iron uptake and increase the risk of iron deficiency.

Common signs of low iron may include:

- tiredness or low energy
- pale skin or dark circles under the eyes
- poor concentration or irritability
- cold hands and feet
- reduced appetite or interest in food
- brittle nails or hair loss
- pica (eating or craving non-food items such as ice, clay, or paper)

 The World Health Organisation notes that serum ferritin is the most reliable marker for assessing iron stores in the body. Low ferritin levels indicate depleted iron reserves.

Importantly, iron deficiency can exist *with or without anaemia* (a low red blood cell count). In most cases, children with iron deficiency can be safely and effectively treated through oral iron supplementation and dietary changes, under medical supervision.

Low zinc and appetite

Fussy eaters are more likely to have lower zinc intake, compared to other children. Insufficient zinc levels may impact appetite as zinc is essential for the proper functioning of taste and smell receptors.[21,22,23]

If your child lacks sufficient zinc, their ability to taste and smell food may be affected, leading to a reduced interest in eating, as discussed in Chapter 6. Zinc also plays a role in mood regulation, and a deficiency can contribute to irritability and behavioural changes.

A lack of zinc can also cause dysgeusia, a condition where taste perception is distorted. Foods may taste different or even unpleasant, discouraging your child from eating and reinforcing food aversions.

Additionally, zinc is essential for growth, and insufficient levels can impact height development.[24]

No appetite and appetite boosters

In rare cases, a paediatrician may consider using an appetite stimulant when a child's appetite remains low despite addressing underlying causes. These medications act on hunger pathways in the brain and body to encourage eating, but their use must be carefully supervised.

Because research on their effectiveness is limited–and their long-term impact on growth and behaviour is still unclear–they are usually reserved for children with specific medical conditions, not for typical fussy eating.[25]

Medical options

Prescription appetite stimulants can temporarily increase hunger or support weight gain, but evidence outside hospital settings is mixed. Some children show mild improvement; others show no meaningful change. Potential side effects–including drowsiness, or irritability–mean these medicines are used cautiously and always as part of a broader plan involving dietary and behavioural support.

Natural approaches

Gentler, natural strategies can sometimes help restore a child's appetite.

- Ginger is a well-known digestive aid used to relieve nausea
  and improve stomach emptying, which can help reduce
  early fullness and encourage hunger. Ginger capsules or teas
  may be discussed with your doctor or dietitian to ensure
  safety and suitability. [26,27]

- Adequate sleep and regular physical activity naturally help balance hunger and fullness hormones, supporting a steadier appetite rhythm.

While these approaches can be helpful, the key is to understand why your child's appetite is low. Identifying and addressing the underlying causes–whether physical, emotional, or sensory–remains the foundation for helping children rediscover the desire to eat.

QUICK REFLECTION

- Where would you place your child on the appetite continuum?
- Does your concern about their eating match what their growth and energy levels are showing?
- Do you need to explore possible factors such as low iron or zinc that might be influencing appetite?

CHAPTER 8

CONTINUUM 3–
EATING SKILLS

Eating is driven by instinct, but it is not a simple reflex. It is a complex learned skill that develops over time. While hunger motivates a child to eat, eating itself requires coordination between muscles, nerves, and the senses, as well as careful timing between breathing and swallowing.[1] From sucking in infancy to chewing and using utensils children develop eating skills through opportunity, repetition, and comfort.

Most children master these skills naturally when given time, positive experiences, and a variety of textures. Delays can occur for many reasons–from early feeding difficulties to medical, motor, or sensory challenges–but with the right support, they can be overcome.

LEARNING TO EAT

Learning to breastfeed

Breastfeeding is one of a child's first eating lessons. It involves coordination of sucking, swallowing, and breathing–the same foundation needed for later eating. Difficulties at this stage may reveal tongue-tie, a high palate, or low muscle tone, all of which can make milk transfer harder.

If breastfeeding was challenging, reviewing those early experiences can help make sense of later feeding patterns.

Learning to manage textures

Solids are usually introduced around six months, alongside signs of readiness such as sitting upright and losing the tongue-thrust reflex, as recommended by the World Health Organization (WHO). [2]

Around 7 months, babies begin learning to handle thicker, mashed and lumpier textures. Spitting food out at this stage is often misinterpreted as dislike, when it is part of developing oral control and learning to manage textures. Gagging is also common in the early stages of learning solids, particularly up to around 8 months. It helps protect the airway while children learn where food should sit in the mouth before swallowing.

As chewing and swallowing skills mature, gagging naturally decreases. If it continues beyond 9–10 months or happens even with smooth foods, it may signal a delay in oral-motor or sensory development and be worth discussing with a speech pathologist or feeding specialist.

Between about 8 and 12 months, children develop the ability to self-feed using a pincer grasp, which involves picking up small pieces of food between the thumb and index finger. They bite off small pieces with their front teeth and move food to the side of the mouth for mashing–an early form of chewing. This is a critical window for learning to manage mixed textures. [3]

As children transition toward family foods, their oral-motor coordination improves. They begin rotary chewing, a circular jaw movement that grinds food more efficiently. By the preschool years, most children manage a wide variety of textures, though they may still need help cutting firmer foods. If they later refuse foods they once ate, the difficulty is rarely due to a lack of eating skills.

Delays with oral-motor skills

Some children struggle with chewing or swallowing due to coordination challenges, sensory sensitivities, or structural differences in the mouth or throat. These children struggle to progress textures. They stay on smooth purees and graduate to crunchy and soft textures. This pattern of food preference often reflects their oral-motor abilities, including tongue movement and the ability to collect and manipulate food in the mouth.[4]

Speech pathologists can assess these skills and recommend exercises or appropriate textures to build strength and confidence.

Talya told me that her five-year-old son is not a fussy eater and enjoys a variety of foods. However, mealtimes can take up to two hours. Throughout the meal, she frequently reminds him to 'chew, chew, chew' as he seems to forget he has food in his mouth. I suggested that Talya see a speech pathologist who specialises in feeding.

Learning to accept taste and flavours

Taste development is a gradual process that begins in the womb and continues throughout early childhood. It is both innate and learned. Infants are naturally drawn to sweetness–an evolutionary trait that once helped our ancestors identify calorie-rich foods essential for survival.[5] Strictly speaking, taste refers to the basic sensations detected by the taste buds (sweet, salty, sour, bitter and umami), while flavour is the broader experience that also includes smell and other sensations in the mouth.

While babies are born with a preference for sweetness, they can quickly learn to accept other tastes such as umami and salty.[6] Sour flavours often require more exposure and practice. Because humans instinctively associate bitterness with potential toxicity, developing a tolerance and eventually an enjoyment of bitter foods can take years.[7]

A baby's sense of taste and early preferences can also be shaped by the flavours their mother consumes during pregnancy and breastfeeding.[8] Genetics play a role too. Some children's taste receptors are more sensitive to bitterness, making certain foods harder to tolerate.[9] Research by Matty Shiva showed that babies with heightened taste sensitivity–hypergeusia–at birth were more likely to become selective eaters by age two.[10]

More recently, Australian researchers have identified another factor influencing taste experiences: the bacteria in the mouth.[11] The oral microbiome produces small amounts of gas that can intensify flavour perception, particularly when eating cruciferous vegetables such as cabbage, Brussels sprouts, or cauliflower. The higher the sulphur production, the stronger the taste sensation.

Families often share similar taste sensitivities, but adults have already learned to tolerate flavours that children are only just beginning to navigate.

Spices and peppery foods add another layer of sensory complexity. These sensations are not detected by taste buds but by the trigeminal nerve, which registers heat, tingling, and coolness in the mouth. Foods containing chilli, pepper, ginger, or even mint can therefore feel intensely 'hot,' 'spicy,' or 'sharp.'

Children with heightened oral sensitivity may experience these sensations as uncomfortable or even painful, while others find them stimulating or exciting as discussed in Chapter 9.

QUICK REFLECTION

- Where would you place your child on the learning-to-eat continuum?
- If your child struggled to breastfeed, were they checked?
- Is your child comfortable with chewing food?
- Did your child previously show strong eating skills, comfortably eating a wide variety of foods before becoming more selective?
- Does your child avoid specific tastes (e.g sour?)

CHAPTER 9

CONTINUUM 4–
SENSORY SENSITIVITIES
AND OVERLOAD

Eating isn't just about taste or smell–it's a full-body experience. Every bite draws on multiple senses working together: what food looks and smells like, how it feels in the hands and mouth, the sounds of eating, the body's balance and posture, and the inner cues that tell us when we're hungry or full. When these systems communicate smoothly, eating feels natural and enjoyable. When they don't, eating can quickly become stressful or unpredictable.

THE CHANGING NATURE OF SENSORY SENSITIVITIES

Sensory sensitivities can change over time and across environments. The same child–or adult–may react very differently depending on familiarity, culture, and exposure. You might remember being bothered by certain textures or smells as a child, only to find they no longer trouble you.

In the same way, two children with similar hypersensitivities to texture may tolerate completely different foods. One might happily eat dhal or chewy rice cakes because they are part of their family's routine, while the other would baulk at such foods.

The environment doesn't create sensory sensitivities, but it shapes how they are expressed and tolerated overtime.

Every child's sensory experience is unique. What matters most is how these sensitivities affect daily life. When they cause distress, avoidance, or interfere with everyday activities like eating they may need extra attention and support.

Sensory food aversion

Sometimes, a single unpleasant sensory experience can change the way a child approaches food. This is known as sensory food aversion–when the brain links a smell, texture, or taste with discomfort or disgust–discussed later in this chapter. From that point, the child's nervous system, reacts protectively, urging avoidance. The reaction isn't behavioural defiance; it's the body's way of saying, 'This doesn't feel safe.'

When we were children, my sister Nathalie would gag and dry-retch at both the smell of milk and the thin skin that forms on boiled milk. There was no way she could drink it. For her, these sensory details weren't minor dislikes–they triggered a strong physical response.

SENSORY OVERLOAD

Think of sensory processing like a volume control that's hard to set just right–this is the sensory continuum in action. For some children, the volume is turned up too high – ordinary sensations feel intense or uncomfortable. For others, the volume is too low–they barely register sensory input and may seek more stimulation to feel balanced.

Sensory overload sits at the far end of this continuum. It describes when the brain has difficulty organising or responding to sensory information effectively. While mild sensory differences can appear in many children, more pronounced dysfunction is most often seen in those with developmental differences such as autism or ADHD.[1]

A useful way to picture this is through the *sensory cup metaphor*. Each child has an invisible cup that fills with sensory input throughout the day. Children who are over-responsive have smaller cups that fill quickly–everyday sensations can spill over into distress, avoidance, or withdrawal. Children who are *under-responsive* have larger cups that rarely fill–they may crave extra movement, pressure, or noise to feel grounded.

When it comes to eating, some of this input travels through the gustatory and trigeminal pathways, which help the brain register taste, texture, temperature, and oral sensations such as fizz, spice, or tingle. These pathways explain why some children find certain foods overwhelming, while others crave bold or stimulating flavours.

Research shows that children with heightened sensory sensitivity at age four are more likely to develop fussy eating behaviours by age six– a reminder that how children process sensation can shape their relationship with food.[2]

When a child's sensory cup overflows, they reach sensory overload. Their brain becomes flooded with more information than it can process, triggering fight, flight, or freeze responses.[3] These moments aren't misbehaviour; they are signs of a system working at its limit.

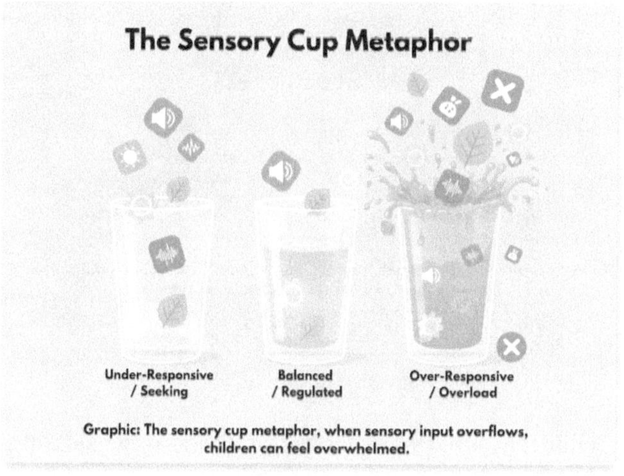

Graphic: The sensory cup metaphor, when sensory input overflows, children can feel overwhelmed.

SENSORY SENSITIVITIES ACROSS THE SENSES

Take a minute to imagine your child at dinner:

- what they see, touch, smell, taste, bite, chew and hear

- the way food feels in their mouth and how they move it around and process it before swallowing
- their body's state during meals, whether they feel hungry, full, restless, tired, anxious, or in pain

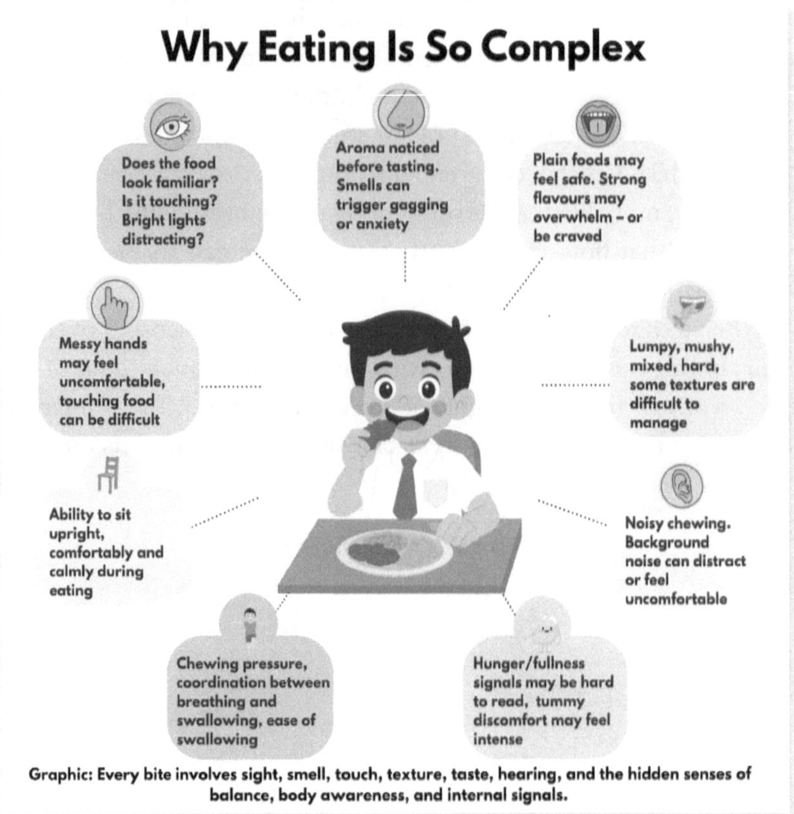

Graphic: Every bite involves sight, smell, touch, texture, taste, hearing, and the hidden senses of balance, body awareness, and internal signals.

Vision

For many children, what food looks like is the first deciding factor in whether they will eat it. Some children rely heavily on visual predictability: they want food to appear the same each time, arranged in a familiar way, and separate on the plate. When things look unexpected or 'wrong' eating can feel unsafe before the first bite.

Children who are visually sensitive may also be unsettled by bright lights, busy patterns, or cluttered dining spaces. For others, the opposite is true–they might not notice visual cues, overlook new foods, or struggle to recognise subtle differences in shape or colour.

Smell

Smell plays a crucial role in our decision to eat, often influencing us before we even see the food. It allows us to detect and identify odours, sometimes from a distance.[4] Think about the inviting aroma of a barbecue as you walk past or, conversely, the unpleasant scent of food on public transport. One may stimulate your appetite, while the other may turn your stomach.

Children who are highly sensitive to smells may experience strong aversions, discomfort, or even gagging, making them over-responsive to certain scents. Some may also develop anxiety around food smells. This is especially common in children with ASD, who often exhibit heightened sensitivity to odours.[5] Children who are under-responsive to smells may not notice odours as readily as others. They might compensate by sniffing foods more frequently and may show less interest in eating overall.

Touch and Texture

Touch and texture are closely connected. The sense of touch allows a child to perceive physical contact–how things feel in their hands, on their skin, and inside their mouth. Texture is the quality of that touch: whether food feels smooth, rough, grainy, sticky, or lumpy.

Children who are over-responsive to tactile sensations may refuse to touch or pick up food and show signs of *tactile defensiveness*. [6] They might avoid feeding themselves, wipe their hands frequently, or react strongly–even gag–when food touches their lips or enters their mouth. They may also be highly aware of temperature or find it distressing to have food on their face or around their mouth.

Because texture is part of touch, sensitivity to certain textures often appears early. Babies, toddlers, and children may reject lumpy purées, mixed foods such as spaghetti Bolognese or risotto, or harder foods like meat, which can gradually narrow their food preferences.

It's estimated that between 16% and 22% of children are texture sensitive. [7]

Under-responsiveness to touch and texture can look quite different. A child might not notice food on their face or hands, fill their mouth too much–mouth pocketing–and forget to eat. These children may seek stronger sensations–preferring crunchy or firm foods that provide more feedback, they may enjoy chewing on non-food items.

Taste

Taste is more than what happens on the tongue–it's how the brain receives and interprets information from taste receptors and related nerves. For some children, this pathway is finely tuned; for others, it's turned up too high or too low, shaping how they respond to flavours and oral sensations.

Children who are over-responsive to taste often experience ordinary flavours as intense or unpleasant. Foods that others find mild may taste bitter, sour, or 'too much.' They may strongly reject peppery, minty, or tangy foods, gag with new tastes, or prefer a narrow range of plain and predictable flavours. These children's sensory systems are quick to register taste input and may struggle to filter it, leading to discomfort or avoidance.

Children who are under-responsive to taste may hardly register flavour at all. They might describe foods as tasting 'the same,' show little interest in eating, or seek extra stimulation through strong tastes and sensations. They may crave salty, sour, or spicy foods to increase oral feedback.

Hearing

Hearing allows us to perceive and interpret sound. Children who are over-responsive to sound may be highly sensitive to noise, reacting with discomfort or avoidance behaviours.

They might struggle to eat in noisy environments, cover their ears, become agitated, or refuse to eat foods that make loud or unpleasant sounds.

Conversely, children who are under-responsive to sound may have a reduced reaction to noise, including minimal response when their name is called.

Interoception–Internal

Interoception is the sense that allows us to perceive what's happening inside our bodies–hunger, thirst, temperature, the need for the toilet, or even emotions such as anxiety or excitement.

It plays a vital role in regulating food intake. Children who accurately interpret cues like hunger and fullness are better able to develop balanced eating habits. For those with interoceptive challenges, including many children with autism or ADHD, recognising and responding to these signals can be more difficult.

Over-responsiveness occurs when children are acutely aware of their internal sensations. For example, they may notice every gurgle or stretch in their stomach and interpret ordinary sensations–such as digestion, gas, or fullness–as pain or distress. This heightened awareness can, for instance, contribute to Functional Abdominal Pain (FAP), where children experience persistent abdominal discomfort without an identifiable medical cause. It reflects an over-responsive interoceptive system, where normal gut sensations are amplified and felt as pain.

Under-responsiveness, on the other hand, means a child may not register hunger, thirst, or fullness until they are extreme. These children might skip meals, eat irregularly, or fail to notice discomfort until it becomes severe. They may also be less aware of the need to use the toilet, which can complicate feeding and digestion.

Vestibular balance

Vestibular senses are responsible for our balance and spatial orientation. When children are over-responsive, they may avoid certain movement activities. However, if they are under-responsive, they may seek intense sensory experiences involving movement.

Children need to be in an optimal position for eating, including having their head in an upright position.

Proprioception–body awareness

Proprioception is the sense that tells us where our body is in space and how much effort or pressure to use when moving. It works alongside the vestibular and tactile systems to help children coordinate movement, maintain posture, and manage physical tasks–including eating.

At mealtimes, proprioception allows a child to judge how firmly to grip utensils, how wide to open their mouth, how much to bite, and how to coordinate chewing and swallowing.

When children are over-responsive, they may be hyper-aware of body sensations or movement. Sitting still can feel uncomfortable, and ordinary sensations–such as food texture or temperature–may feel too intense.

When they are under-responsive, body sensations register weakly. These children may appear floppy, fidgety, or constantly seeking movement, and they can find mixed textures or coordinated chewing difficult to manage.

Because proprioception interacts with several other senses, challenges in this area often overlap with tactile or vestibular sensitivities.

> Four-year-old Leo used to sit with his head down, watching a favourite cartoon on mum's phone while he ate. He coughed regularly as food particles went down the wrong pipe (aspiration). With his low muscle tone, watching a screen while eating created a hazard for him.
>
> Without a screen, Leo can sit upright. His mother decided that screen time would be offered after meals. Initially, Leo threw a few tantrums but once he knew the routine, he relaxed. Sitting upright, he doesn't cough anymore.

Speech-Language Pathologists (SLPs) and Occupational Therapists (OTs) can help children find balance–where there are sensory hyper-sensitivities.

QUICK REFLECTION

- Where would you place your child on the sensory continuum?
- Are they comfortable sitting, or do they fidget?
- Does your child struggle with textures, smells, taste or even the way food looks to the point where they become dysregulated?
- Does your child avoid chewing?
- Does your child seem not to feel hungry at all?

CHAPTER 10
CONTINUUM 5–FOOD NEOPHOBIA AND DISGUST

As children grow, two instinctive protective reactions often appear around food–neophobia and disgust. Both are part of normal development and serve to keep the body safe from potential harm.

FOOD NEOPHOBIA–A NORMAL STAGE

Food neophobia, the reluctance to try new foods, is a normal developmental stage that sounds worse than it is.[1] It typically begins around 18 months of age and can appear suddenly: a child who once ate everything may start pushing food away, smelling it first, or picking at it before deciding whether to eat. Rejection of both new and familiar foods can occur on sight alone.[2]

Up to 75% of children go through this stage.[3] It's part of gaining independence and learning to approach food with caution–a leftover survival instinct that once protected humans from eating unsafe foods

For most children, food neophobia sits on the typical end of the fussy-eating continuum. It usually peaks between two and six years of age and fades by around eleven or twelve.[4, 5]

However, for some children, this stage is more intense or lasts longer. [6, 7,8]. Contributing factors can include:

- greater sensitivity to taste or texture
- medical problems or discomfort with eating
- temperament, such as shyness or low approach or heightened caution
- higher levels of worry or vigilance around new or unfamiliar experiences
- early feeding struggles or limited exposure to a variety of food[9, 10, 11, 12, 13]

When several of these factors overlap, food neophobia can be more challenging–but it is still part of a child's normal development.

DISGUST

Disgust is an emotion designed to protect us from contamination and disease. It often appears alongside food neophobia and in many children it is the driving emotional force behind strong or persistent refusals. Foods that touch or are mixed together commonly trigger this reaction–the classic 'yucky!' response.

When we encounter something we perceive as dirty, dangerous, or potentially harmful, the brain triggers a disgust response that helps us avoid or reject the threat.

This protective reaction is useful–it keeps us safe–but it can also make eating uncomfortable when triggered too easily or strongly.

Smell, sight, and touch play key roles in disgust, helping us rapidly judge whether food feels 'safe'. For children with sensory hypersensitivities, these cues can register more intensely, meaning disgust responses are triggered faster and more strongly. This can lead to strong or long-lasting aversions driven by disgust or fear of contamination. Mixed foods–or foods touching on the plate–are common examples.

As researcher Paul Rozin noted, disgust is 'probably the most intuitive of all the emotions'.[14] It helps us avoid harmful substances. It can also arise from non-physical triggers such as thoughts, memories, or associations. A child might feel sick at the idea of a food even when it's not in front of them, reflecting learned threat responses in the brain and body rather than the actual safety of the food.

Disgust is also learned and shaped by culture. Foods considered normal or even desirable in one culture can be seen as repulsive in another–as illustrated by the dietary boundaries of traditions like kosher or halal eating.

QUICK REFLECTION

Where would you place your child on the continuum of food neophobia and disgust?

CHAPTER 11

CONTINUUM 6–
TEMPERAMENT AND EATING

'My child is very stubborn.'

It's a phrase many parents use when describing their child's fussy eating–often followed by words like strong-willed, rigid, or sensitive. These words capture not just behaviour at the table, but deeper differences in how each child experiences and responds to the world.

Temperament influences how a child eats just as much as how they sleep, play, or adapt to change. It shapes their comfort with new foods, reactions to unfamiliar textures, and ability to stay calm when routines shift. Understanding your child's temperament can help you interpret their behaviour at mealtimes–and choose approaches that work *with*, rather than *against*, their natural tendencies.

Since the 1970s, psychologists have recognised temperament as a key part of child development. Much of it is genetic–something children are born with, not something parents cause. Although personality grows and changes with experience, temperament itself stays relatively stable over time.[1]

You may have heard of the classic categories of temperament–*easy*, *difficult*, *slow to warm up*, and *active*. These can be helpful for understanding broad patterns, but most children don't fit neatly into one box. Instead, they fall along a continuum of traits that interact with their environment. The calm, cheerful child next door likely has what researchers call an *easy temperament*–not necessarily a better upbringing, just a different starting point.

Recognising these natural differences can be deeply reassuring. Temperament is not a reflection of your parenting, but an opportunity to understand your child's needs more clearly–and to adapt the mealtime environment so it supports their individual wiring.

 Oscar and Alice are siblings. Alice, who is ten months old, wakes up smiling, goes to sleep easily, and is learning to eat solids with ease. Her parents can take her to restaurants, settle her in the pram, and she drifts off to sleep happily. Alice has an easy temperament.

Oscar never slept well as a baby. At four years of age, he often has meltdowns when changes occur in his day. Mealtimes are challenging, as he eats only a limited variety of foods and prefers familiar brands he recognises. On paper, Oscar shows a more difficult temperament.

TEMPERAMENT CHARACTERISTICS AND FUSSY EATING

Studies have shown that children with a difficult temperament–characterised by negative emotionality, low soothability, and high impulsivity–are more likely to be fussy eaters.[2] Temperament, however, is made up of several interacting traits, each of which can influence eating in different ways.

Emotionality

High negative emotionality may indicate your child is more prone to anxiety, fear and distress, leading to reluctance to try new foods.

Soothability

A low score means your child may have difficulty calming down or regulating their emotions. They may become upset or distressed if they don't want a particular food and may have difficulty calming down afterwards, even once the meal has ended.

Sensory sensitivity

Children who are highly sensitive to sensory stimuli may find certain tastes, smells, or textures overwhelming, which can make eating more challenging. As discussed in Chapter 9: Sensory sensitivities and overload, these responses are linked to how the body processes sensory information, rather than to behaviour or preference.

Impulsivity

If your child is highly impulsive, they may react quickly once a food lands on their plate. Because they don't take time to assess the situation, they might brush off the food or dismiss it before giving it a chance. This can make mealtimes unpredictable, especially when new foods are introduced. Impulsivity often overlaps with attention and self-regulation challenges, making it harder for children to pause and adapt in the moment.

Activity level

A high level of activity means your child may have difficulty sitting still or focusing during mealtimes. A low level of activity may translate into a smaller appetite, while still being within the range of what the child needs.

Adaptability

If your child has low adaptability, they may have difficulty adjusting to new situations and experiences as well as to changes in routine. This can extend to becoming distressed or anxious when presented with new or unfamiliar foods.[3] For example, they may become distraught if the meal is not what they expected or if it's served in a different setting or with different people.

Approachability

If your child is hesitant or cautious in new or unfamiliar situations or settings, their level of approachability is low. These children often come across as timid and need time to warm up to new situations and environments. When it comes to food, they may refuse it multiple times before they try it.

Distractibility

If your child is easily distracted by toys or other stimuli, such as their reflection in the window, they may lose interest in their food. They may have difficulty sitting still or following rules during mealtimes, particularly if this pattern becomes established. Children with ADHD are more likely to have feeding difficulties and selective eating behaviours.[4]

> Jay is very distracted at meals; he loves to watch his reflection in the kitchen windows and pays very little attention to the food in front of him. It's crucial to optimise his appetite to ensure he eats better at mealtimes. To help him eat more effectively, his parents now remove distractions and close the curtains so he can focus on his meal.

Every child's temperament shapes how they approach eating—whether with enthusiasm, caution, or resistance. These patterns aren't fixed or 'good' or 'bad'; they simply show how your child is wired to respond to the world. Recognising their temperament helps you make sense of mealtime behaviour and prepares you to support change in a way that feels realistic and compassionate.

QUICK REFLECTION

Where would you place your child on the temperament continuum?

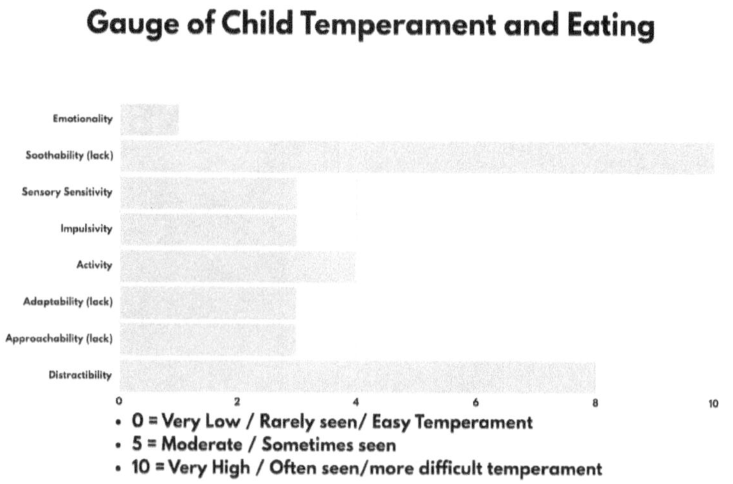

Gauge of Child Temperament and Eating

- 0 = Very Low / Rarely seen/ Easy Temperament
- 5 = Moderate / Sometimes seen
- 10 = Very High / Often seen/more difficult temperament

Graphic: the higher the child's sensitivity and intensity, the greater the likelihood of fussy eating responses.

CHAPTER 12
CONTINUUM 7–ANXIETY AND STRESS RESPONSES

All the continua we've explored so far–from appetite and sensory processing to temperament, medical discomfort, and disgust–converge here. When these systems are under strain, a child's body may begin to treat food as a potential threat, triggering the body's protective fight, flight, or freeze responses. Over time, repeated discomfort or distress teaches the nervous system to expect danger. What began as sensitivity or pain becomes fear and avoidance–the roots from which anxiety around food can grow.

ANXIETY IS NORMAL UNTIL IT GETS IN THE WAY

A certain amount of anxiety is a normal and even helpful part of life. It can keep us alert, help us prepare for something new, and signal when something doesn't feel right. For children, it's natural to feel anxious about unfamiliar experiences–like trying a new food or eating away from home.

> Five-year-old Sammy refuses to go to sleep by himself. His parents lie down with him and usually exit the room

once he is asleep, but recently he has started to wake up and call them. At dinner, Sammy becomes distraught when there's new food on his plate. School drop-offs can also be challenging, and he has started to complain about tummy aches.

But anxiety exists on a continuum. For some children, anxiety appears as mild worries or clinginess. For others, anxious thoughts become more persistent, rigid, or overwhelming, sometimes meeting criteria for conditions such as Generalised Anxiety Disorder (GAD) or Obsessive–Compulsive Disorder (OCD).

When anxiety becomes intense or ongoing, it can begin to shape a child's relationship with food and feeding. Children might worry about the taste or texture of food, whether it's cooked the 'right' way, or how it will feel in their mouth. Some may fear gagging or vomiting. Others may have no words for the discomfort at all–only a strong, instinctive urge to escape.

 Seven-year-old Sarah's parents would love to eat out, but it has become increasingly difficult over the years. Now Sarah worries, 'What if there's nothing I can eat?'

Her parents try to reassure her, but anxiety always wins. Eventually, it feels easier not to go at all–and that's why restaurants no longer feel possible.

This is where anxiety meets the body.

THE THREAT RESPONSE: FIGHT, FLIGHT, OR FREEZE

When a child feels overwhelmed, their brain may interpret food as a threat, activating the body's threat response. This response is often expressed as fight, flight, or freeze. The amygdala, the brain's alarm system, floods the body with stress hormones such as adrenaline and cortisol, preparing it to respond. This response is often behind what looks like 'defiant', 'rude' or 'rigid' behaviour at the dinner table. But it's not bad manners–it's survival mode.

This is not a time for learning. When the body is in survival mode, appetite shuts down. Even sitting at the table may feel too much. Once their nervous system begins to calm, some children will return to eat. Others may stay heightened and skip the meal entirely.

Recognising signs of overwhelm

These stress responses aren't always obvious. Meltdowns, sudden loss of appetite, or emotional outbursts are often clues that your child's nervous system is overwhelmed. And because young children's prefrontal cortex–the part of the brain responsible for regulation–is still developing, it's harder for them to self-soothe or explain what they're feeling.

So, it helps to put on your 'detective hat' and observe. What does your child do when something is too much? Are they truly defiant, or might they be scared? Are they fussy, or are they flooded?

HOW THE THREAT RESPONSE SHOWS UP

Once you understand that a child's refusal, avoidance, or distress at the table may be a threat response, it becomes easier to respond with empathy rather than frustration. Let's look more closely at how this might show up in different children.

Fight

Some children move into offence mode. They argue, cry, demand, or insist that the food isn't 'right'. You might hear, 'There's nothing to eat' or 'It tastes weird'. What looks like rudeness or a need for control is the body's way of regaining safety when food feels unpredictable or unsafe. In that moment, their system is flooded: they're not reasoning, they're reacting.

Flight

In the flight response, the child simply tries to get away from the food, the pressure, or the discomfort they feel. They might leave the table, appear restless or highly distracted–watching a screen–or refuse to join family meals altogether. Some avoid eating in social settings. Others turn into entertainers, using humour or charm to divert attention. What looks playful is often a strategy to escape discomfort–a way of keeping both themselves and their parents safely away from the real challenge of food. In flight, the child is still highly activated–their system is busy getting away.

> Seven-year-old Sebastian is sitting better at mealtimes and appears more relaxed. This evening, his father, mid-bite, looks at him and exclaims, 'This is so yum!' In an instant, Sebastian bursts into laughter and runs away from the dinner table.
>
> 'Did you see that flight response?' I ask Sebastian's dad.

Freeze

Some children respond by completely shutting down. They may look vacant or shut down at the table, with very little energy to engage. Appetite seems absent, and parents often step in to take responsibility for the eating–offering reminders, coaxing, or feeding bites themselves, worried their child will otherwise not eat at all. The child isn't being passive; they've checked out. What looks like calm or compliance is actually overwhelm. A calm child isn't always a comfortable child. Unlike flight, freeze isn't about escape–it's about survival through shutdown.

MELTDOWN OR TANTRUM?

When a child reaches their limit in their threat response, behaviour may escalate into a meltdown, as if the amygdala has hijacked the nervous system. This is not the same as a tantrum.

- Tantrums tend to happen when a child wants something they can't have. They're goal-driven, and usually end once the need is met–or the child realises it won't be.
- Meltdowns, on the other hand, are not controlled. They occur when a child's nervous system is flooded. This might be triggered by sensory overload (as discussed in Chapter 9), a sudden change in routine, or intense anxiety–especially around food.

A child in meltdown is not trying to manipulate or defy. They are overwhelmed and unable to cope. Because every child's stress system is wired a little differently, meltdowns can look very different from one child to another.

Food related meltdowns can involve fighting or escaping depending on how the child's nervous system responds. Some children may gag or even vomit. Others may need a while to recover and sit down at the dinner table.

Even as children grow and develop better self-regulation skills, meltdowns can still happen– especially for those who are neurodivergent. Our job isn't to stop the meltdown. It's to recognise it for what it truly is: a nervous system in distress. Once we see it that way, we can focus on helping children feel safer and calmer–reducing the chances of future meltdowns and gently paving the way for more positive food experiences.

ANXIETY, FEAR, AND AVOIDANCE

By now, we've explored how anxiety can affect appetite and how the threat response can shut down a child's ability to engage with food. What often follows is avoidance–not a behavioural choice, but a physiological escape from distress.

Avoiding food isn't about being difficult. It's the only strategy a child has in that moment to feel safe from the intense sensations or fears triggered by food. For children with sensory sensitivities, medical discomfort, or a history of distressing feeding experiences, avoidance works—it brings instant relief. But that same relief reinforces avoidance.

Fear around food can stem from many experiences: a choking episode, an overwhelming smell, a difficult texture, or simply the unfamiliarity of a new food. When those experiences trigger a threat response, food stops being food—it becomes a perceived danger. By now the amygdala is on constant alert around food. It learns through experience, and this is what it has learned.

Avoidance then becomes a survival tactic. Over time, it can appear as rigidity—a child insisting on sameness, resisting change, or refusing to eat unless everything feels predictable. To manage that anxiety, children often draw their parents into the pattern. Meals may slowly shift to revolve around 'safe' foods, specific routines, or strict rules that help the child—and the family—feel calmer in the moment.

This process, known as *accommodation,* is deeply understandable. It reduces distress in the short term but also keeps the child's nervous system from learning that food can be safe again. Over time, both parent and child become locked in a cycle of protection—one seeking to feel safe, the other seeking to preserve calm.

BRINGING THE SEVEN CONTINUA TOGETHER

Now that you've explored each of the seven continua, take a moment to reflect on where your child might fall across them.

The example graph below shows how feeding challenges can range from mild to more complex, depending on how many areas are affected and to what degree. It offers a visual snapshot of your child's unique feeding profile.

Remember: there are no right or wrong answers, the aim is insight, not a score. If your child experiences a combination of factors–such as medical discomfort, delayed oral-motor skills, sensory sensitivities, anxiety, or temperament differences–their fussy eating may be more complex, and seeking professional guidance can provide clarity and support.

You are not alone. Many families I work with have children who feel anxious at mealtimes, struggle with texture, or experience strong food neophobia and disgust. A significant number of these children also have autism, ADHD, or both. Extreme fussy eating is never a simple issue–it is a web of valid struggles, not a reflection of poor parenting or a child being difficult on purpose.

You've now stepped into your child's world and begun to see

eating through their eyes. That understanding is powerful–and it is where real change begins.

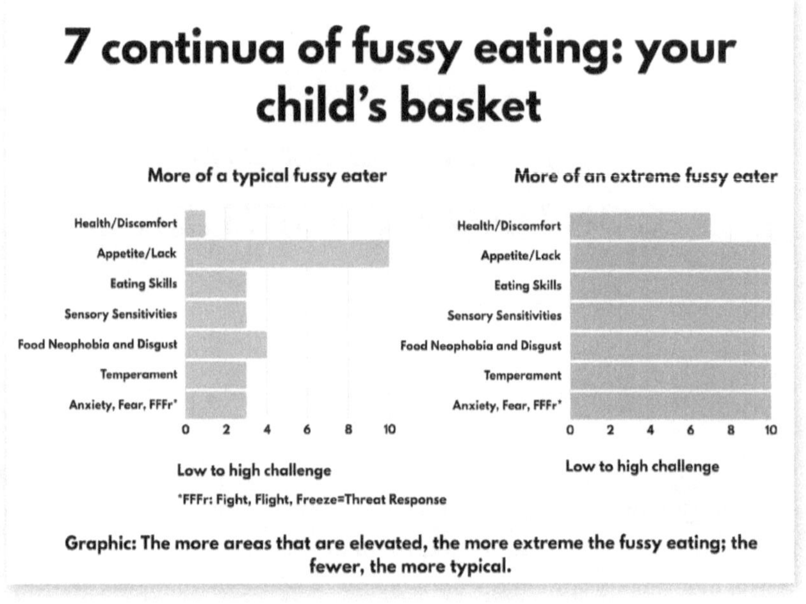

Graphic: The more areas that are elevated, the more extreme the fussy eating; the fewer, the more typical.

SECTION 3: THE REBOOTS

By now, you've seen how many different factors–health, appetite, sensory sensitivities, temperament, anxiety, and more–can shape a child's relationship with food and eating. When fear or discomfort arises, the body reacts with fight, flight, or freeze responses, leading to avoidance–and the child becomes caught in that loop.

At times, it can feel as if everything is stacked against your child.

But here's the truth: even in complex circumstances, parents have an enormous influence. You can't change your child's biology or temperament, but you can create the environment they need to feel safe, calm, and curious about food again.

Research by Dr Eli Lebowitz and his team at the Yale Child Study Centre shows that parents tend to respond in one of two ways to a child's anxious avoidance: they either dismiss it or accommodate it.

In feeding, this shows up clearly. When we dismiss a child's struggle with a food, we push harder to get them to eat it–and it backfires. When we remove the food altogether, we reinforce fear and avoidance. That backfires too.

Now that you understand what's going on, you're ready to take the first steps on the middle path–neither dismissing nor accommodating. This is where the Reboots begin.

HOW LONG WILL IT TAKE TO SEE PROGRESS?

I can hear you asking: *'How long will it take before my child actually eats new foods?'*

It's a completely natural question.

Along the way, you will see progress. Your child will learn to sit more comfortably, to relax, to settle into the routine, and most importantly, to feel calm at the dinner table. Mealtime meltdowns often reduce and may gradually disappear, and you begin to show your child that they can step outside their comfort zone safely, without activating the threat response.

But the truth is, for children with long-standing or intense feeding difficulties, this deeper progress takes time.

I often ask parents: 'Would you expect your child to excel at piano after just a few sessions?'

Of course not. Even the most gifted child needs practice, repetition, and confidence before the music starts to flow.

Learning to eat is much the same. It's a complex skill that unfolds gradually, step by step, as your child's body, nervous system, and confidence grow.

The most powerful thing you can do is trust the process and let your child feel that trust. When you become confident that you've 'got this', your child senses it. Your calm, steady leadership becomes the signal their body needs to relax, explore, and, in time, take steps towards new foods.

CHAPTER 13

REBOOT 1–BUILDING THE FOUNDATIONS FOR CALM EATING

As we move into the first Reboot, remember what we discussed at the start of this book–each Reboot builds on the one before it. This first step is the essential foundation for everything that follows.

Here we focus on your child's feeding routine and environment–the building blocks that create safety, predictability, and the appetite needed for progress.

By the end of this Reboot, you'll have a solid routine that supports genuine hunger and helps your child feel physically comfortable, settled, and ready to eat. Your goals for this stage are to help your child:

- come to the table hungry
- sit comfortably and securely
- relax and follow the mealtime routine–joining the table, staying seated, and transitioning calmly when the meal ends

THE HUNGER RHYTHM

A child's appetite plays a crucial role in their eagerness to eat. While some children clearly signal when they're hungry, others show few signs, making it difficult to tell when they need food.

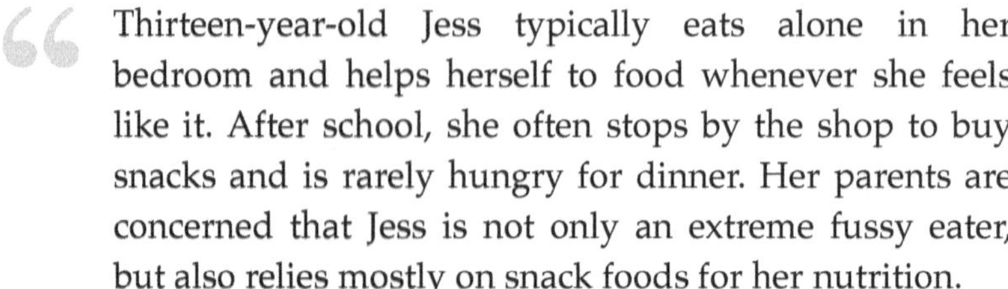

Thirteen-year-old Jess typically eats alone in her bedroom and helps herself to food whenever she feels like it. After school, she often stops by the shop to buy snacks and is rarely hungry for dinner. Her parents are concerned that Jess is not only an extreme fussy eater, but also relies mostly on snack foods for her nutrition.

But hunger doesn't have to be a mystery. When meals follow a consistent rhythm, your child's body begins to *predict* when food is coming. The hunger hormone ghrelin, as discussed in Chapter 7, rises in anticipation of a meal, not just once eating begins.[1,2] Over time, a steady mealtime schedule teaches the body when to prepare for eating.

That's why grazing interferes with appetite. It prevents ghrelin levels from cycling properly. In Australia, almost all children (99.8%) have at least one extra snack a day–snacks that can blunt appetite and weaken the hunger needed to engage fully at the next meal.[3]

It's okay for your child to feel a little hungry between meals, it is a healthy body cue, not a sign of deprivation. When meals and snacks are predictable, your child's body can regulate appetite and relearn when to feel hungry.

This is not restriction either. Snacks still have an important place. They are simply offered at set times rather than on demand. The same applies to milk feeds, which also benefit from structure. Excessive milk drinking can dull appetite for solid food.[4] For toddlers, milk is best limited to around one or two cups–up to 500 ml–a day, ideally offered with meals or snacks rather than between them.

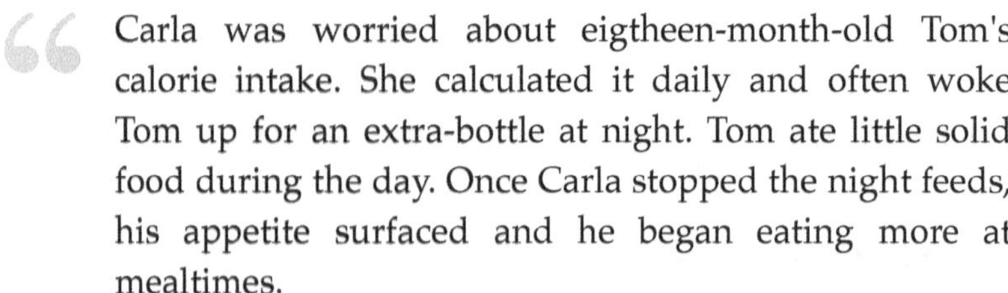

Carla was worried about eigtheen-month-old Tom's calorie intake. She calculated it daily and often woke Tom up for an extra-bottle at night. Tom ate little solid food during the day. Once Carla stopped the night feeds, his appetite surfaced and he began eating more at mealtimes.

If your child still has a night bottle, it may be time to phase it out. Night feeding often suppresses daytime appetite. Once those feeds are reduced, you'll likely see genuine hunger return for breakfast and main meals.

 Ben's mother developed a habit where she offers him a snack whenever he sits in the car or the pram. However, it's hard for her to tell when Ben is ready to eat, as he rarely seems interested in food. She is also concerned she is using food to soothe him or to get his compliance.

What is a strong routine?

A strong daily routine fits your child's needs around meals, sleep, and everything in between—and helps *you* feel confident and in charge.

A strong routine:

- **Is predictable**: As your child learns their routine, they feel reassured that food comes at regular times. Predictability helps both of you relax and find your rhythm.
- **Includes clear transitions**: Meals have a clear start and finish, helping children understand when the kitchen is open and when it is closed.
- **Helps regulate appetite**: Regular routines teach the body to anticipate food, supporting consistent hunger cues and calmer mealtime.
- **Builds lifelong self-regulation and agency**: When children follow consistent routines, they learn to pause, show up, and take part—skills that later become the foundation for independence, from preparing meals to managing their own eating with confidence.
- **Is delivered with confident direction**: You'll find more detailed examples of language and scripts for structure and transitions in Chapter 16.

Your mealtime routine

Consider offering 4 to 6 meals a day with gaps in between.

Start by setting the main meals–breakfast, lunch, and dinner–with about five to six hours between them. The word *about* gives helpful flexibility, especially for children who fixate on exact times and may become distressed if meals don't occur precisely on schedule.

For example:

- breakfast at about 7:30 am
- lunch at about 1:00 pm
- dinner at about 6 pm

Once these three mealtimes are established, keep them consistent. You can add snacks halfway between meals, but the main mealtimes should stay firmly in place.

While you'll shape your routine around your child's needs and your family's rhythm, here are a few examples to guide you.

Scenario 1: for a child attending early learning or school.

- breakfast at about 7:30 am
    - snack at about 10:00 am
- lunch at about 1:00 pm
    - snack at about 3:30 pm
- dinner at about 6:00 pm

Scenario 2: for a toddler with a midday sleep and a late breakfast.

- breakfast at about 8:00 am
- lunch at about 11:00 am
- sleep at midday
    - snack at about 2:30 pm
- dinner at about 5:30 pm

Scenario 3: for a child who eats poorly during the day or takes ADHD medication.

- breakfast at about 7:00 am
- snack at about 10:00 am
- lunch at about 12:30 pm
- snack at about 3:00 pm
- dinner at about 5:30 pm
- supper at about 8:00 pm

In some families, it can be a good idea to move dinner to afternoon snack time. Your child may pay more attention to dinner if they are hungrier at 4:00 pm.

- breakfast at about 6:30 am
- snack at about 9:30 am
- lunch at about 1:00 pm
- dinner at about 4:00 pm
- supper at about 6:30 pm

SITTING AS A LEARNING CONDITION

Supporting your child's ability to sit properly during meals is crucial for successful eating. Good sitting promotes comfort, focus, and confidence–and it's a skill every child can learn. Since children need to sit well at childcare and school, introducing this early makes a lasting difference.

With consistent practice, your child can gradually increase their seated mealtime duration –starting with just five minutes and extending up to 20–30 minutes.

To achieve this, three factors matter most:

- Hunger as a motivator. If your child isn't hungry, they won't feel motivated to sit at the table.
- Proper ergonomics for comfort and support. Imagine perching on a bar stool with no footrest, unable to see your food properly–eating would soon feel like work. Your child's seat should be stable, well-supported, and appropriately sized so they can sit upright, see their food

easily, and reach it without lifting their elbows or straining forward.

- A relaxed state for learning. If your child feels stressed or overwhelmed, they may enter fight, flight, or freeze responses, making it impossible to learn about new foods.

Every family's setup looks different–some eat at the dinner table, others at the kitchen bench, and some on the floor. Whatever your space, the goal is the same: your child should feel stable, comfortable, and able to focus on eating. Proper support helps them stay still, enjoy food, and feel more independent.

Seventeen-month-old Daniel dislikes being strapped into his baby chair. With his legs dangling, he spends mealtimes kicking the chair rather than focusing on eating.

Five-year-old Lea sits on a booster seat attached to an adult chair, but the seat tilts backward, causing her to slouch. To eat, she awkwardly lifts her shoulder and elbow just to scoop food onto her spoon.

Seven-year-old Jack uses an adult chair, but during meals, he fidgets constantly shifting from sitting to kneeling and struggling to stay comfortably seated.

Nine-year-old James finds it hard to stay still during meals. He climbs on and off his chair and runs around, which makes it difficult for him to focus on eating. However, at school, he uses a wobble cushion, which helps him stay engaged while seated.

When sitting well makes eating easier

When it comes to feeding, where your child sits matters more than most parents realise.

Poorly fitted seating can lead to fidgeting, slouching, or fatigue and make eating harder work than it needs to be.

- **Baby chairs**: Toddlers often outgrow them around 18 months. Once strapped in, they can feel restricted and frustrated.
- **Booster seats**: While convenient, they rarely provide enough support. Children tend to slouch, dangle their feet, or struggle to sit upright.
- **Adult chairs**: Too large for most children under nine or ten, leaving them constantly adjusting, fidgeting, or tiring quickly.

An adjustable chair designed for children's comfort and ergonomics can transform mealtimes.

These chairs:

- grow with your child through early adolescence
- provide adequate foot, back, and hip support
- help align posture and jaw for easier eating
- retain strong resale value once you're done with them

Many include attachments for babies and toddlers, making them a sound long-term investment.

If cost is a concern, you can look for second-hand options–many families sell or give them long before their usefulness ends.

Parents who make the switch often describe the difference as 'transformational'.

They notice calmer behaviour, better focus, and more comfortable eating almost immediately.

Children often take pride in their new chair. Encourage ownership–let them choose the colour or decorate it with stickers. Calling it a 'big kid chair' can also help with acceptance.

As a parent, you set the tone. Make the new chair part of the mealtime routine and a consistent expectation–it's one more way to bring calm and confidence to your table.

Extra support for wriggly eaters

If your child struggles to stay still, you can add sensory aids such as a wobble cushion or a fidget band around the chair legs. These allow gentle movement while keeping your child seated and engaged.

Before you give up on sitting

Many parents struggle to help their child sit for meals–sometimes to the point of following them around with food. But don't give up on sitting–I've seen time and again that children eat better when they sit well.

> Gemma's parents remind her: 'sit properly, another five minutes.' Gemma scans the table then grabs another piece of fruit and keeps eating.

If your child struggles to sit, it's worth pausing before jumping to techniques. Understanding why they resist sitting helps guide what to do next.

Here are some common reasons, and what they can tell you:

- Not hungry. Without hunger, there's no motivation to sit or eat. That's why we're implementing a routine. If appetite remains low despite routine, consult your doctor for further assessment, including iron status (see Chapter 7, Continuum 2–appetite).
- Many children simply don't know what 'sitting properly' means. Clear, brief expectations given ahead of time can help children understand what is expected of them. Practical examples of this language are covered in Chapter 16.
- Restless or under-stimulated. Some children need more physical movement and sensory input during the day to help their bodies regulate and be ready for mealtimes. Include some active play or calming movement in their routine so they can settle when it's time to eat.

- Tired or overstimulated. A child who's tired may become irritable, fidgety, or withdrawn at meals. Consider an earlier dinner or a short rest before mealtime. After school and afternoon snacks, plan some quiet downtime before dinner.
- Deeply focused on another activity. Transitions are hard when a child is engrossed in play. Use simple time cues like 'Now you play, then in 10 minutes it's dinner.' Visual schedules or timers can help. Once seated, allow a few minutes for them to shift into eating mode.
- Needing time to process what's coming for dinner. For some children, the challenge isn't sitting itself, but having too little time to process the meal before sitting down. A short buffer before meals can help, see Chapter 15.
- Reliance on screens. Some children won't eat without a screen. While screens can reduce anxiety or distract from sensory discomfort, they also disconnect the child from the experience of eating. Explore what's driving the need–unclear expectations, sensory issues, or anxiety–before phasing screens out gradually or moving them to another part of the day.

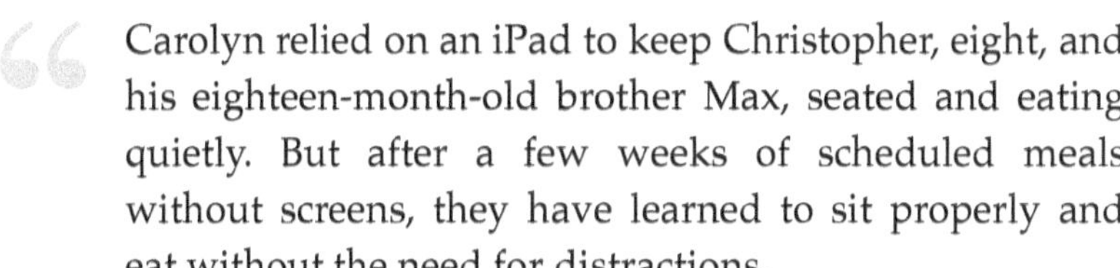

> Carolyn relied on an iPad to keep Christopher, eight, and his eighteen-month-old brother Max, seated and eating quietly. But after a few weeks of scheduled meals without screens, they have learned to sit properly and eat without the need for distractions.

- Fight, flight, or freeze responses. As you've learned earlier, these reactions can surface around food. When a child sees something on their plate as a threat, they may run away, shout, or shut down. This isn't defiance–it's a fear-based reaction, the body's way of saying, 'I don't feel safe right now.' When fear takes over, appetite switches off. Focus first on calm and safety; return to the table once your child feels regulated again.

 Eight-year-old Elle sat in the car on the way home from school saying, 'I don't want a cooked dinner, I want W!'* Her father tried to reassure her: 'We have pasta and sausages, which you like. You'll be fine.' But Elle repeated her preference for W* over and over again, in an increasingly agitated tone. When her parents served the meal, Elle unravelled and began begging for W*. Her parents tried to negotiate their way out of this down-ward spiral: 'Have some pasta first, then you can have some W.' That evening ended with Elle screaming and crying as she ran away from the table. Her parents found her curled up on the sofa. Desperate, they finally offered the breakfast cereal she had been asking for since 3 pm. W* = a brand of breakfast cereal.

Understanding this behaviour is key. Elle had shown signs of fatigue and sensory overload after school. She wasn't throwing a tantrum; she was overwhelmed and on her way to meltdown. Her statement that she did not want a cooked dinner was a clear indicator that she could not cope with the sensory demands of flavours and textures in a cooked meal, while her body urgently sought calories in a quick, predictable form. Elle's flight response had taken over–not something she could be rational about. Once Elle became familiar with the Meal System (see Reboot 2), meltdowns became a thing of the past.

Communicating routine and sitting through voice, visuals, and touch

Even with a strong routine and good sitting support, some children still resist sitting at the table. Once you've ruled out hunger, tiredness, or fear, calm communication can help reinforce expectations.

Communication around sitting often works best when voice, visuals, and physical guidance are aligned:

- **voice**: short, calm instructions that signal confidence

- **visuals**: cue cards, visual schedules, and pictograms can help children understand what's expected
- **physical guidance**: gentle support to help a child organise their body

You'll explore how to use these tools in detail in Chapter 16. For now, focus on consistency rather than perfect wording.

You can give the feeding environment a fresh feel and signal that something is changing by swapping seating positions at the table or introducing new cutlery or placemats.

> Jordan, a lively three-year-old, now sits calmly at meals. His parents consistently guide him back to his chair using calm voices and a simple visual prompt. Sometimes they gently hold his hand to help him return to the table; other times, when they sense he's about to move, they show the visual cue first and say, 'Sit properly.' Occasionally, they just help him readjust to a better sitting position.

INITIATING RELAXATION

By putting the strategies from this Reboot into practice, you're beginning to create the first level of mealtime relaxation. With a steady routine and comfortable sitting, your child knows what to expect, and appetite begins to appear at the right time. The table feels quieter, movements slow down, and there's your sigh of relief.

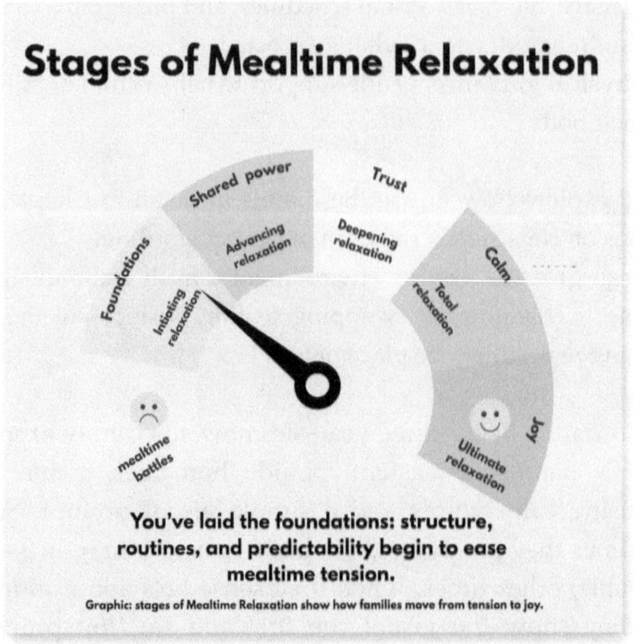

You've laid the foundations: structure, routines, and predictability begin to ease mealtime tension.

Graphic: stages of Mealtime Relaxation show how families move from tension to joy.

REBOOT 1: LET'S GO!

Observe

- Does your mealtime routine need to be adjusted?
- Do you need to stop your children from grazing between meals?
- What can you do now to implement ergonomic sitting? Do you need an adjustable chair?
- Are there behaviours around mealtimes, such as good sitting, that you could improve using visual, verbal, or physical prompts.
- Are there times when you use food to soothe, distract, or reward your child rather than to meet hunger?

Take action

1. Review seating arrangements.
2. Review your mealtime routine.
3. Decide whether you will use visual, verbal, or physical prompts to communicate your expectations.

Assess progress

After working through Reboot 1, stand back and reflect on what has changed.

- Where have you and your child been successful?
- What still needs work?
- Is there anything you tried that didn't work–and what can you do instead?
- How do you feel?

Reboot	Progress Check-list 1	
1	Parent are nailing transitions and routine	☐
	Child's appetite is showing at mealtimes	☐
	Child's seating arrangement is ergonomic	☐
	Child sits better	☐
	Child knows when kitchen is open or closed	☐
	Child starts to relax knowing food is offered at regular times	☐

Building the foundations for calm eating

REBOOT 2–SHARING POWER WITHOUT LOSING YOUR ROLE

Have you ever told your child 'one more bite for me'–and felt it was harmless, even encouraging?

You're not alone. Most parents use a little pressure now and then, believing it helps their child eat better.

In a podcast conversation with Amelia Phillips, host of *Healthy Her*, she shared how some pressure seemed to work well with her own children. And for many families, especially when children are naturally compliant, it can seem harmless.

But for the families I work with, the story is often different. When a child is sensitive, anxious, or stubborn, even gentle pressure can have the opposite effect, increasing refusal, distress, or anxiety at the table.[1,2]

What feels like encouragement to a parent can feel like pressure to a child whose body is already on alert, in a fight, flight or freeze response. Their push-back may look like stubbornness, arguing, or tears–but it's their nervous system saying 'I don't feel safe right now.'

Some of the pressure tactics we'll explore here may reflect the parenting styles discussed in Chapter 3. For example, a more controlling style may rely on stronger prompts or insistence, while a more permissive approach may use coaxing or negotiation. Regardless of the style behind it, however, pressure is still pressure from the child's perspective.

Now that the structure and routine from Reboot 1 are in place, this is the moment when removing pressure and sharing power can truly take effect. It is the step that changes the emotional climate at the table and lays the groundwork for trust.

In this Reboot, we'll look at how pressure undermines eating, and how sharing power instead builds trust and progress at mealtimes. You may already sense that pressure feels wrong–tightening the moment rather than opening it.

By the end of this Reboot, you'll have strategies to help you:

1. remove all pressure from meals
2. share power with your child
3. build trust

REASONS FOR PRESSURE

It's only natural to feel frustrated when your child suddenly refuses a dish they once loved, or turns down a new food that seems simple enough.

For many parents, there's a quiet tug-of-war inside: one part of you believes pressure is necessary, while another part feels guilty or unsure. This conflict alone is a sign of how deeply you care.

Parents often apply pressure because it:

- Feels logical and familiar: it's a food they have enjoyed before or one that seems simple and familiar enough to manage.
- Creates a sense of control in a situation that can feel unpredictable or stressful and offers momentary relief. Applying pressure can feel like taking action rather than standing by helplessly.
- Reassures you that you're doing your job as a parent, supporting your child to eat well and stay healthy.

- Draws on your own experience with food. You know what tastes good, what feels safe, and what your child needs to thrive.
- Stems from concern that without prompting, your child may not eat enough quantity or variety.
- Is fuelled by your own nervous system. When fear, worry, frustration, or urgency rise, pressure can feel instinctive or automatic.

But your child's experience is completely different. Children don't eat because something makes sense to parents; they eat when their body feels ready and safe enough to do so. To help them move forward, we need to reduce threat responses and allow children to reconnect with their internal motivation to eat. Research consistently shows that intrinsic motivation, rather than external pressure, fosters long-term positive eating habits.[3]

Graphic: Parental logic versus child's body contributes to applying pressure

When pressure sneaks in without us noticing

Because pressure often feels caring or helpful, it can slip in without us realising. Parents are usually trying to encourage, guide, or support their child to eat, not to create stress. Yet even well-intentioned prompts can become pressure.

Pressure exists on a spectrum, from subtle nudges to more obvious tactics. What matters is not how gentle it seems, but how it is experienced by the child.

As you read the list below, see if you recognise any forms of pressure that might show up at your table. Then ask yourself what feels familiar. This isn't about blame, but awareness.

- Is pressure working?
- How does my child respond to it?
- How do I feel about using it?
- Does it help build trust around food and mealtimes?
- Is my child learning to enjoy food?

Graphic: Pressure, even in disguise, is pressure

Verbal praise and cheering

Praise and cheering often sound warm and encouraging, but both can quietly create pressure. A 'Well done!' or a round of applause may seem harmless, yet it sends the message that eating is a performance. Children start to eat to please you rather than listening to their body's cues.

When praise or cheering becomes routine, children can start to feel anxious about meeting expectations. You may also notice your child looking to you for approval before taking a bite, or waiting for praise afterwards.

Emilia is sitting in her high chair, eating with her spoon and stopping to clap her hands. Will her mother clap too? As Emilia takes a bite, her mother Yvette gives her rapturous applause: 'Well done, you're such a good girl!' She then places mashed potatoes on Emilia's plate, but the sixteen-month-old is quick to throw the food on the floor, screaming and kicking her legs. Yvette is puzzled. She tries hard to keep Emilia happy at meals and thinks it may be time to remove challenging foods.

Asking too many questions

Parents may unintentionally create pressure by offering too many choices or asking too many questions about food. Children have limited experience with food and may struggle to make decisions, particularly if they're tired or unsure. Constantly asking, 'What do you want to eat?' or 'Why don't you like it?' can overwhelm them. Often, they simply don't know.

When these questions stem from parental anxiety, children tend to mirror that anxiety, making mealtimes even more challenging.

I'm spending the weekend away with my niece and her eighteen-month-old daughter, Ciara. I've heard that little Ciara can be a fussy eater. Some of her father's childhood feeding struggles still linger, and I remember the tension that often surrounded family mealtimes when he was young.

One morning, Ciara becomes upset, running anxiously back and forth to her mother's arms. Her mother keeps asking, 'What do you want to eat?'–but each question seems to heighten Ciara's distress.

When I'm invited to help, I suggest a different approach. Instead of asking questions, I encourage her mother to prepare a few breakfast items while I sit Ciara beside me, gently patting her back until she begins to calm.

As the food is placed within reach, Ciara picks up a few raspberries and grapes. I notice her watching her cousin's porridge, so I place a small bowl of thick porridge near her–close enough to explore, but not on her plate. She examines it carefully, tastes a little, then spits it out. I stay calm and relaxed. Mixing some yoghurt with the porridge, I take a bite myself. Ciara looks intrigued and amused–then offers to feed me.

When she finally tries the porridge and yoghurt mixture, it becomes clear that finding a food she would eat wasn't the issue after all. With calm structure and emotional steadiness, Ciara begins to co-regulate with me, allowing curiosity to take the place of anxiety.

Pre-plating and the illusion of control

Pre-plating can create a false sense of control for parents. The logic seems simple: if the peas are on the plate, the child is more likely to eat them.

However, for anxious or fearful children, this isn't exposure–it's an avoidance cue. The sight of unwanted food can trigger discomfort or refusal. Rather than encouraging progress, pre-plating can backfire and reinforce food-related anxiety.

Alex tells me he makes sure his son Joshua has exposure to peas as he places them on his plate almost every day. Joshua takes one look at his plate, runs away and refuses to come to the dinner table.

Is this exposure or harassment by peas?

Smelling, licking, and tasting requests

It's easy to want to nudge your child forward and ask them to smell, lick, or take a small bite of food. These steps can seem harmless, even therapeutic, but they often reflect the parent's need for progress rather than the child's readiness.

When parents slip into the therapist role, mealtimes can become strained and feel unnatural, increasing the risk of pressure and complicating both feeding and the mealtime relationship. Remaining in the role of parent and focusing on connection rather than compliance is not only simpler, but more effective.

> I am sitting with parents, Luke and Jen, their fussy eater Will, and toddler Oscar.
>
> 'Oh look,' says Jen, 'Dad is eating carrot. He'll see in the dark!' Four-year-old Will ignores the comment, while his younger brother giggles. 'Dad, can you pass me the rice?' Jen asks in an exaggerated sing-song voice. 'Here it is! How many spoons for you, Dad?' Then, turning her attention to Will, she continues, 'What's in the rice? What can you see, Will? I like the smell of corn. Can you smell it too?' Will isn't interested. He leaves the table several times throughout the meal. At the end of dinner, both parents tell me that ever since Will had feeding therapy, this is how they create 'happy mealtimes.' They are exhausted.

Playing the role of enthusiastic, animated eaters after a long workday feels unnatural and draining. More importantly, it isn't working.

Just one bite

Just one bite?' or 'I'd love for you to give it a try.' It sounds reasonable—not pushy, just a small ask. The hope is that tasting the food will lead to liking it.

But for many children, that single bite feels anything but small. They resist, pushing back even harder. And when they finally take a bite, it's often followed by a quick, 'I don't like it,' which brings the interaction to a halt.

For some children their threat response triggers gagging or vomiting.

This raises an important question: is eating a piece of carrot worth the distress? If a child gags or vomits, will they ever willingly eat that food again?

Playing eating games

Do you race your child to a bite of food? Have you ever created an eating board game? Parents exhibit unlimited creativity when driven by the desperation to get food into their child.

Sometimes, I pretend I'm going to steal his food. And sometimes, he jumps in to help himself and stop me. I have to say, it doesn't work all that often, admits David, father of nearly three-year-old Lucas.

Selling a benefit to eating

Should children eat food because it's tasty or because they're hungry?

When we suggest that food serves purposes beyond hunger and enjoyment, we turn eating into a transaction. Naturally, children begin to question whether the food is enjoyable. In a society where discussions about healthy eating dominate, parents often try to persuade children to eat by linking food to health benefits.

Interestingly, studies show that when food is associated with a promised benefit–such as 'This cracker is healthy'–children tend to eat less of it. The same effect occurs with messages like 'It makes you strong,' 'It helps you read,' or 'It is yummy.' Rather than encouraging eating, these statements can backfire, making children more sceptical and less interested in the food.[4]

Statements like 'If you want to grow strong like Daddy, you need to eat your meat' or 'If you eat carrots, you will see in the dark' rarely convince children. Often, they reply with something witty, such as 'But I don't want to grow' or 'I'm a vegetarian,' instantly shutting down the attempt.

Children quickly recognise and counter these types of pressure-driven tactics. Interestingly, if you look at how food products are marketed to children, you'll notice playful characters and bright packaging, that's it. Offering food without attaching conditions or benefits is more effective in encouraging a positive relationship with eating.[5]

Bribes and rewards

'If you eat your broccoli, you can have some chocolate mousse.' It sounds familiar–and it may work in the moment–but it comes at a cost.

Using food as a reward teaches children that eating is transactional. They learn to value the reward dislike and distrust the 'required' food even more.[6], [7,8] Over time, this approach can fuel fussy eating and emotional overeating of the reward food, rather than trust and curiosity. [9]

Distraction

Screens, toys, or songs may distract your child long enough to sneak in a few extra bites, but this bypasses awareness and self-regulation. When children become aware they can clamp their mouth, they learn to push back or simply lose interest in eating.

Scrutinising your child's plate

Do you stay silent about your child's eating during meals but find your eyes constantly scanning their plate? Do you check in real-time how much and what they are eating? Many parents develop this habit over the years, often without realising it. However, your child notices–and feels it.

Comparing and encouraging siblings

Comparing a child's eating to that of siblings or other children can unintentionally increase pressure, especially when it happens in front of them. When parents hope comparison will motivate a fussy eater, or ask older children to encourage a sibling to eat, the effect is often the opposite. Children may feel inadequate or discouraged by not being able to eat like others, which can deepen resistance rather than support progress.

Arguing and mocking

It's easy to reach breaking point and find yourself arguing with your child over food. Arguments often begin when parents try to convince their child to eat their way. In frustration, these exchanges can escalate into mocking or belittling remarks about their eating habits.

Emotional blackmail

Parents sometimes feel unappreciated for the effort, care, and love they put into meals. Their child's refusal can be particularly painful. As a result, one or both parents may beg their child to eat the food 'for Mum' or 'for Dad', using appreciation and love as talking points.

Using scare tactics

Parents naturally worry about their child's nutrition and long-term health. In a culture that emphasises 'we are what we eat' and closely scrutinises our child's plate, it's easy to slip into warning or even threatening a child about the consequences of their limited eating.

Sarah and Brandon joined me on a video call. 'It's hard to admit, but we've resorted to scaring Josh,' they confessed.

'We tell him monsters will come and get him. It's the only way he'll eat his veggies. He screams the house down at dinner–every single night.'

Physical containment and force-feeding

Sometimes, especially with younger children, parents feel desperate for their child to eat and may gently hold their child in place while feeding them. This can look like sitting behind a child, wrapping an arm around their back or waist, and bringing the spoon in with the other hand.

For the child, this can feel overwhelming: their body is restricted and escape isn't possible. Eating becomes associated with fear rather than safety. It is particularly risky when a child leans back to avoid the spoon, as their airway is less protected–even a single cough is a sign that their body feels unsafe.

Punishing

When parents fear losing control, or when their beliefs about what a child *should* eat are reinforced by an authoritarian style, they may tighten control instead. This can lead to punishing a child by sending them to bed on an empty stomach or insisting they finish everything on their plate before leaving the table.

> John shares a video of dinner with his two children. 'Julia, just eat four peas so we can move on,' he says, exasperated. Kate, his six-year-old, finishes her meal with ease, but Julia, nine, has struggled with food for a long time. 'It's not that hard,' John sighs. 'Kate's done, and you're staying here until you've had those four peas.'

THE CONSEQUENCES OF PRESSURE ON TRUST

Imagine taking a bite of food and being praised every time, how would that feel? Now, picture yourself hesitating to try a plate of snails, a French delicacy, and instantly facing a stream of questions about why you won't give it a go. What would the pressure of eating a scary food feel like in your own body?

Then, imagine every meal filled with constant chatter, encouragement, scrutiny, and any other form of pressure we have discussed. Day after day, meal after meal, with eyes fixed on you, would it start to feel overwhelming? Would your body feel the anxiety not just at meals but before them? Would you ever trust that meal can be pleasant and stress-free?

Children who experience pressure may lose trust around food and mealtimes, arriving at the table expecting tension rather than calm. They may push back by arguing. They may dysregulate with meltdowns, refusing to sit, making excuses to leave the table, pushing food away. They may stop recognising their own appetite cues. Or they may simply switch off and passively accept being fed.

Older children may develop clever tactics to escape eating. I've seen parents sit for hours, begging their child to eat, only to end up eating the food themselves in frustration. And for the children including teenagers who do push themselves to take a bite under pressure, they later tell me they never end up liking that food. For them, the taste becomes tied to stress, not curiosity–and certainly not trust. It's another quiet way pressure backfires.

Consider the pressure you have at your disposal. Does it genuinely help? Does it support your child in trying new foods, or does it create more resistance? Most importantly, how does it make you feel?

> Ben's mum sighs in frustration. 'I swear you'll love this. Just have a go, it's really yum! Don't you trust me?' Ben looks up and, without hesitation, replies, 'No, Mum, I don't trust you.'

REMOVING PRESSURE, SHARING POWER, AND BUILDING TRUST

When parents remove pressure from mealtimes, they take a huge step toward helping their child move past fussy eating. This is about sharing power without giving it all away, and finding balance. Parents provide structure and set the mealtime environment, while children decide whether and how much to eat.

The *Division of Responsibility (DOR)*, developed by Ellyn Satter, is considered the gold standard in feeding. It's endorsed by organisations such as the American Academy of Paediatrics, Nutrition Australia, and the Dietitians of Canada, and its principles are reflected in national child-feeding guidance across New Zealand and the United Kingdom.

As discussed in Chapter 3, cultures such as France naturally embody these principles through structured, shared meals where parents decide *what, when,* and *where* food is served, and children are trusted to decide *whether* and *how much* to eat–a cultural expression of balance, trust, and pleasure in eating.

At its heart, DOR is built on trust: parents trust their child to learn to eat, and children trust that meals will be predictable, calm, and pressure-free. It benefits the whole family by reducing stress, easing anxiety, and making mealtimes more enjoyable.

Trust is the only currency you have when feeding your child. It tells them, 'I believe you can manage your eating, and I'll stay calm while you do.' Every mealtime is an opportunity to bank trust–or lose it.

Graphic: building trust at the dinner table

APPLYING THE DIVISION OF RESPONSIBILITY (DOR)

Simply put: *you decide what, when, and where; your child decides if and how much.* Once the food is on the table, your role is complete and your child takes it from there.

Lucy thought her daughter was too thin. She felt responsible for every bite five-year-old Ella took. Then, she noticed that pushing Ella to eat resulted in more pushback and less eating.

After three months of applying DOR consistently and correctly, Ella started to eat greater quantities. She was also showing more curiosity about food and was happier at mealtimes. Lucy was relieved as she had managed to release the burden of responsibility she'd been feeling around Ella's eating.

You are not responsible for your child's food intake.

If you've already implemented Reboot 1, you've established where feeding happens and when it happens. Now it's time to focus on 'the what'–your Meal System.

The Meal System

Each meal is a system made up of two food categories: the main and the staples. As children experience repeated meals structured this way, they gradually learn how the Meal System works.

Mains usually involve some preparation and form the centre of the meal. Staples are familiar, reliable foods that can be added easily from the fridge, freezer, cupboard, or fruit bowl. Together, they create a predictable structure that supports both appetite and confidence.

Within the Division of Responsibility (DOR), all food is viewed as neutral. This matters more than it might seem, because no food carries more virtue or value than another. When meals are structured this way, pressure reduces and children are able to tune into hunger and fullness without fear or judgement.

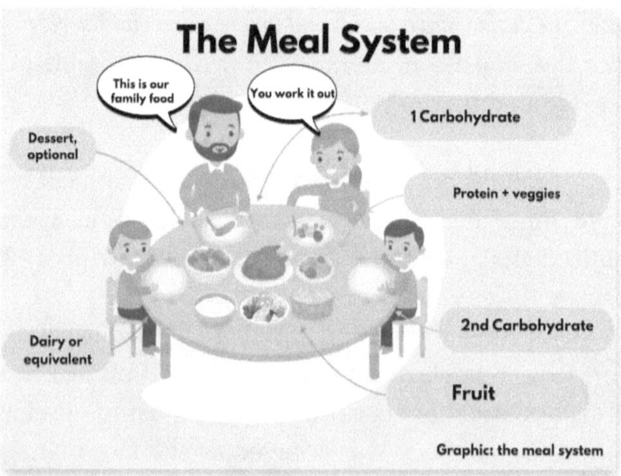

Graphic: the meal system

Examples:

- In a traditional Indian meal, a spread might include rice and roti, chickpeas or chicken with vegetables curry, yoghurt sauce, spiced fruit salad, and a dessert such as Barfi.
- In France, meals are typically served in courses. Children might be offered crudités–raw veggies with dressing–first, then a main dish with pasta, followed by yoghurt, fruit, and bread throughout.

Whether served all at once or in courses, the principle is the same: all foods are part of the Meal System. Food remains on the table for children to explore at their own pace, until the kitchen is closed.

A family's interpretation of the meal system

As a dietitian, I have helped plan canteen menus for French schoolchildren. One clear rule we give canteen staff is that bread is always available and unlimited. All food is placed on the table for self-serving. Bread plays an essential role in reassuring children and helping them feel satisfied, while they learn to eat alongside their peers.

The foods that make everything else possible

Staples provide comfort and predictability. Bread, fruit–fresh, frozen, or dried–yoghurt, and cheese are familiar, easy options. They reassure children that they can eat successfully, which in turn frees them to explore new foods.

Before

Clara came home from school famished and anxious, yet as soon as she sat at the dinner table, her appetite disappeared. A single glance at her plate was enough to make her tense and uneasy.

Shift

Her parents changed their approach. Instead of saving dessert as a bargaining chip, they began offering a variety of foods–including dessert–neutrally and all at once, without pressure or conditions.

After

Clara started to relax. Knowing dessert was simply part of the meal, she grew calmer, more trusting, and even began serving herself. With pressure gone, she became more willing to explore other foods alongside the ones she found safe.

Main meals and family food culture

Most families think of the main meal as the central dish they've prepared, usually built around a protein with sides. In many some households, that might look like 'meat and three veg'. In other families, it might be a curry served with rice, a pasta dish shared at the table, or a one-pot meal everyone eats from the same bowl.

Regardless of what it looks like, the main meal plays a key role in shaping a family's food culture. Food traditions are influenced by personal preferences, values, and cultural background, and children learn what *family food* is through repeated exposure over time.

Food acceptance is strongly shaped by early exposure and cultural context–even among children with autism and extreme fussy eating. In families from Indian backgrounds, I have met autistic children who readily eat dhal. In Chinese families, autistic children may accept prawns with ease. In Anglo families, foods like Vegemite often play that same familiar, grounding role.

Serving traditional meals, even when children aren't ready to eat them, builds familiarity by allowing these foods to be experienced as part of everyday family life.

STEPPING BACK SO YOUR CHILD CAN STEP FORWARD

Family-style service is a leap of faith for many parents. You've already seen how pre-plating creates pressure and can trigger the threat response. Here, the key is simply to take the next step: placing the food in the middle of the table and letting your child decide what goes on their plate.

It can feel as though you're giving up control, but in reality, you're removing the trigger that was fuelling rigidity and avoidance in the first place. When children choose what to take–even if it's only bread at first–they stay calmer and more available for learning.

Before

At four, Carlo was beginning to settle into mealtimes. But one slip in approach could undo the calm. One evening, his dad, Ryan, said: 'He's gone off yoghurt lately, so I don't offer it.' Then, turning to Carlo, he asked directly, 'Would you like some yoghurt?' Carlo screamed 'No!' and burst into tears.

Shift

I suggested Ryan stop asking direct food questions, which as we discussed often feels like pressure, especially for tired or sensitive children. Instead, I encouraged him to place yoghurt on the table with quiet confidence, as part of the meal.

After

Minutes later, Carlo spotted the yoghurt, helped himself, and ate without fuss. Being able to see the food, rather than process instructions or questions about it, allowed him to choose in his own time. Ryan realised that how food is presented–calmly and without words–can matter as much as the food itself.

Graphic: family-style service

Plating food for a child can trigger resistance, while family-style service builds confidence. Food no longer comes to the child or at the child. Instead, the child leans forward to engage, shifting the entire feeding dynamic.

This simple change is empowering. It leads to fewer meltdowns and a calmer table for everyone.

THE ROLE AND BENEFITS OF FAMILY MEALS

Modern lifestyles can be busy and hectic, and many parents feel like they don't have sufficient time to eat together as a family. While daily shared meals may not be realistic, even a few shared meals each week can make a meaningful difference. Weekend breakfasts, lunches, or dinners often provide the easiest, most natural opportunities to sit together.

What matters most is not frequency but consistency.

Modelling eating for babies and children

Eating meals together as a family provides an excellent opportunity for parents and caregivers to model eating to babies and children.

When we are born, our brains are equipped with a remarkable feature known as mirror neurons. These specialised neurons are like tiny mirrors within the brain, firing not only when we perform an action but also when we witness someone else performing the same action. This mirroring effect, from which mirror neurons derive their name, enables babies and children to learn by observing and imitating the actions of those around them.[10]

After reviewing countless mealtime videos, one thing has become clear to me: children watch their parents eat. By observing, they learn which foods are safe and how to interact with them. Babies are captivated by a parent's mouth full of food, studying how it moves and processes each bite. This natural curiosity can spark an interest in solid foods during weaning and encourage self-feeding as they grow.

This nonverbal communication method involves parents demonstrating positive attitudes and actions towards food, rather than relying solely on verbal instructions. By adopting a 'do as I do' approach, parents can positively influence their children's eating behaviours.

Parents who model eating to their children report them to be less fussy.[11] Furthermore, these children are more inclined to taste the 'traditionally disliked' vegetables and exhibit increased consumption of fruit and vegetables.[12]

 June was feeding herself, but her mum, Julia, couldn't hide her growing concern over how few foods the eleven-month-old would accept. To ease the pressure, we removed the tray from the highchair and brought June to the dinner table, sitting her opposite her mum.

Julia placed loaded spoons of purée and finger foods within reach, sometimes sharing a plate so they could pick and choose together. She exaggerated her chewing, opening her mouth wide to show an eager and amused

June how it worked. Soon, mealtimes became more relaxed. As Julia and her partner chatted, June explored new foods at her own pace–without any pressure.

Socialising and bonding

Sharing meals as a family is more than just eating together–it's a chance to connect, talk, and bond. It creates a routine that makes everyone feel like they belong, strengthening relationships in the process.

Mealtime conversations encourage open communication, making family members feel supported and heard. This kind of connection boosts emotional well-being and brings a positive energy to the home.

Plus, learning to share meals teaches kids an important life skill. As adults, they'll need to navigate social situations around food–whether it's a date, a business lunch, or a dinner with friends.

Building resilience

It's amazing how much kids absorb about their family's history and values just by sharing meals together. These moments create a sense of stability, strengthen parent-child relationships, and reinforce the feeling of belonging.

Psychologist Marshall Duke has shown that children who regularly share meals with their families develop greater resilience and overall wellbeing.[13] Family meals are associated with lower rates of depression, suicidal thoughts, substance use, eating disorders, smoking, and risk-taking behaviours such as violence or delinquency.

Other benefits

For young kids, chatting at the dinner table helps build vocabulary even more than being read to.[14] And the benefits don't stop there–older kids who have regular family meals tend to do better in school.

On top of that, eating together encourages healthier food choices, helping kids develop good eating habits that last a lifetime.

WHAT TO EXPECT WHEN ADOPTING DOR

Children often test boundaries to see if trusting their parents is worth it. That's why progress with eating new foods can feel painfully slow— or even non-existent–at times. And yes, that can be incredibly frustrating.

Parents need to stay the course and be on the lookout for hidden pressure in every part of their feeding journey. The key is to support each other, spot when pressure creeps in, and stop it before it takes over.

As Ellyn Satter puts it, this phase takes *nerves of steel.* It also helps to master the art of staying silent and keeping a confident, calm expression that says: 'You've got this.'

Your persistence and acceptance that feeding isn't about quick fixes will carry you through.

What if my child will only eat bread, yoghurt and fruit?

It's normal for children to stick to their favourite, easy-to-eat foods at first. They need a solid mealtime routine to build confidence in eating and trust that parents will stick to their role–without pressure.

Liam, a four-year-old boy, used to eat only peanut butter sandwiches for lunch and often had meltdowns when offered anything else.

When we began Food Familiarisation at the bench, Liam showed curiosity about new foods. He tasted cheese and ham and continued to enjoy familiar items like bread and yoghurt. Using these foods as a base, we combined what he already liked with the foods he had explored at the bench. During the week, when interacting with those foods, his parents informed him that his next lunch would include them. This gave Liam time to process the change and feel prepared.

At our following session, Liam sat calmly and fed

himself. The peanut butter sandwich meltdown was over.

KNOWING WHEN TO END THE MEAL

Parents following the Division of Responsibility (DOR) oversee the ending meals and letting children know when the next one will be. If a child is hungry, seated comfortably, and understands the mealtime routine, they should be able to eat within 20 to 30 minutes.

If your child gets distracted or wants to leave the table, you can use an exit plan:

1. Prompt them once more to sit down.
2. Assess their appetite: 'I can see you're playing with your food now; have you had enough to eat?'
3. Affirm: 'The kitchen will be closed until…'

When they're ready to leave, ask them to clear their plate–either placing it on the kitchen bench or in the bin. This helps reinforce that the meal is over. If they later ask for more food, remind them: 'The kitchen is closed until…'

Some fussy eaters take longer to eat due to a range of factors outlined in Chapter 6. In these cases, further assessment may be needed to rule out underlying challenges.

EATING OUT WITH CHILDREN

Many parents find it stressful, wasteful, or simply too expensive to take fussy eaters out to dinner. But learning to eat out–whether at a friend's house, a café, or a restaurant–is an important life skill.

Your child will manage these outings better when expectations are familiar. Until they're older, use the same Division of Responsibility (DOR) approach and Meal System, with you taking responsibility for ordering. Placing food in the middle of the table and sharing can make meals feel familiar and predictable.

Using your shared language–see Reboot 4–you can prepare your child by setting expectations, discussing possible challenges, and practising flexibility.

Timing is key–plan the outing when your child isn't overtired or overly hungry to keep things positive. Many restaurants offer interactive dining experiences, including teppanyaki, sushi trains, Korean cook-your-own meals, and Italian make-your-own pizza. There's plenty to explore and enjoy!

ADVANCING RELAXATION

Letting go of pressure is the single most powerful step you can take toward creating a calm mealtime. When parents release the weight of 'getting their child to eat,' their own nervous system settles–and children settle with them. This is co-regulation in action: your calm becomes their calm.

As you put this Reboot into practice, you're creating a structured, pressure-free environment where your child–whatever their temperament–can feel safe and capable. Clear roles emerge: parents provide; children decide. From that clarity, trust begins to grow, and with trust comes genuine relaxation.

Trust feels steady and pleasant to sit with.

You'll start to feel it: meals that once felt tense begin to soften. The air feels lighter, conversations flow more easily, and your child approaches food with a little more ease and curiosity.

For families whose children have frequent mealtime meltdowns, this Reboot lays the foundation for lasting change. As pressure decreases and safety increases, meltdowns steadily reduce, preparing the way for later Reboots to help resolve them altogether.

This transformation often unfolds gradually–just as it did for Jonah and his family.

Before

Mealtimes in Jonah's home were a source of dread. His parents described the tension as 'walking on eggshells'–never knowing which food might spark outright refusal, tears or anger. They often felt guilty, wondering if they were somehow making things worse.

The Shift

Through the Reboot, Jonah's parents began to strip away pressure and share power. It wasn't about getting Jonah to eat more in the moment, but about building trust and reducing anxiety.

After

Over time, Jonah started approaching food with curiosity instead of fear. He still had preferences, but mealtimes no longer felt like battles. His parents described a newfound sense of relief: 'The stress lifted. We could finally enjoy sitting at the table together again.' Jonah began trying small 'speckles' of food, on his own terms, and slowly added more variety to his diet.

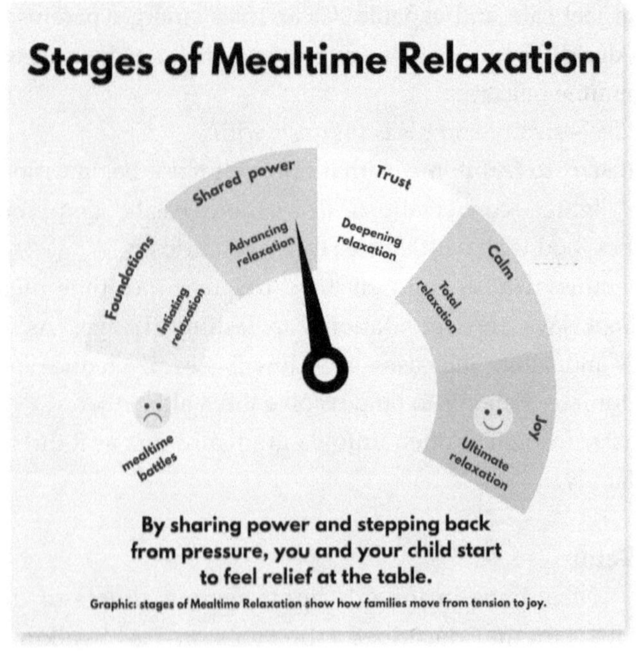

Graphic: stages of Mealtime Relaxation show how families move from tension to joy.

REBOOT 2: LET'S GO!

Observe

- Are you using pressure at mealtimes? Which forms of pressure are you using?
- Are you ready to share power and give your child more autonomy?
- Do you know what to serve, or do you short-order cook what your child requests?
- Do you place specific value on some foods versus others?

Take action

1. Repeat this to yourself: 'I trust my child to manage their own food intake.'
2. Talk it through with your partner. How will you support each other in staying neutral about food and applying DOR?
3. If pressure creeps back in, how will you notice it and call it out kindly?
4. Pay attention to how your stress levels change as you begin sharing responsibility in feeding.
5. Keep your meal structure steady. Your routine from Reboot 1 remains the foundation for success.
6. Be clear about your Meal System and offer food with confidence; it reassures your child.

Assess progress

After working through Reboot 2, take a step back and reflect.

- Where have you and your child made progress?
- What still needs work?
- Did something not go as planned? What can you do instead?
- How do you feel?

This is a learning process–adjustments are part of the journey.

Reboot

2

Progress Check-list 2

Parents identify pressure and understand impact on trust ☐

Parents apply DOR, and are neutral about food ☐

Child is empowered to self-serve ☐

Child is learning Meal System ☐

Child relaxes knowing they can eat successfully ☐

Reduction of dinner time meltdowns ☐

Sharing power without losing your role

CHAPTER 15

REBOOT 3–FROM REFUSAL TO FAMILIARITY

THE FOOD FAMILIARISATION APPROACH

By now, you've laid the foundations for mealtimes: routines are in place, children are sitting comfortably, and pressure is no longer driving the interaction. With this groundwork in place, you're ready to begin what I call Food Familiarisation–my approach to helping children feel at ease with food in all its sensory aspects: how it looks, smells, feels, and eventually tastes in everyday life.

Unlike clinical desensitisation, which often relies on staged exposure tasks, Food Familiarisation is woven into ordinary parenting. It's not about asking children to touch, smell, or taste on command–those requests often create pressure and resistance. Instead, it's about parents modelling calm curiosity: preparing, serving, or talking about food in a relaxed, natural way, while children quietly absorb the experience.

This approach is purposeful, not random. We don't just cook anything for the sake of activity–we choose foods your child isn't yet eating and build skills around them. In this way, desensitisation happens with the very foods that matter most for your family.

Over time, these ordinary, pressure-free exposures reduce the threat response, fear and avoidance. Confidence grows step by step, until readiness and appetite naturally follow. When a child voluntarily brings food closer to their mouth or takes a bite, it's a sign of true comfort. Spontaneity is the clearest marker of real progress.

By the end of this Reboot, you will:

1. understand the three key goals of Food Familiarisation
2. choose specific foods to work on
3. plan Food Familiarisation activities

THE THREE GOALS OF FOOD FAMILIARISATION

Food Familiarisation has three key goals, all designed to support a child's growing relationship with food, whether that means preventing the early formation of a 'fussy eater' identity or gently challenging it in children where it's already taken root. By focusing on skills, confidence, and calm exposure, we help children see themselves as capable and curious, rather than fearful or avoidant.

1. Help food feel safe through sensory engagement: This goal is about regulation, not eating. When the nervous system feels safe, curiosity can emerge.
2. Build problem-solving skills and increase flexibility: This goal is about helping children learn that food is workable, not all-or-nothing.
3. Build confidence through food skills: This goal is about agency, mastery and making food work for the child.

Let's explore these goals in more detail.

Goal 1: Help food feel safe through sensory engagement

Children explore the foods you select at their own pace. There are no expectations to smell, lick or bite. Simple acts of preparation provide natural, multi-sensory exposure and gently support desensitisation.

When children engage in this relaxed way, their nervous system begins to adapt. Food that once felt threatening becomes more familiar, helping quiet the fight, flight or freeze response and allowing children to tolerate its presence without triggering fear or avoidance.

As comfort grows, curiosity often follows, and many children gradually become more open to tasting on their own accord.

When ten-year-old Wilson cuts a tomato, he experiences it in multiple ways. He feels the skin, flesh, seeds and juice under his fingers. Molecules are released into the air, reaching his nose and activating his sense of smell. In that moment, he has engaged with the tomato through sight, touch, sound and smell, and even a hint of flavour. All of this happens naturally and effortlessly, without anyone asking him to smell, lick or bite.

Tactile engagement: the first step to managing Textures

Research by experts such as Helen Coulthard shows that tactile play can reduce food neophobia.[1] Handling foods allows children to explore their texture, giving them information about what that food might feel like in their mouths.

However, some children experience extreme sensitivity to touching food. These tactile defensive children may become distressed if their hands feel messy.

A gradual approach works best. Start with dry foods that are easier to tolerate, such as rice, pasta or oats, and slowly introduce stickier or wetter textures as tolerance builds.

Grading activities: from easy dry to challenging wet foods

Olfactory engagement: a physical and cultural environment

Ever noticed how a fresh food market has a mix of strong, distinct smells, while a supermarket smells like very little at all? Supermarkets are highly sanitised, whereas markets surround you with raw, natural food smells, some fragrant, some intense, and some that take getting used to.

The places you take your child, whether a bustling market, a quiet supermarket, or a fragrant kitchen, shape their awareness of and comfort with different smells. Your home environment matters too. The foods you cook, the spices and herbs you use, and your cooking methods all help build familiarity with food aromas.

Gradual exposure is key. Being in the kitchen while food is chopped, mixed or cooked allows aromas to build slowly, giving the nervous system time to adjust. In contrast, walking into a room filled with a strong smell can feel overwhelming.

Gustatory engagement: the Speckle Method

Feeding therapist Marsha Dunn Klein has highlighted how offering food in tiny bits can ease overwhelm for sensitive children. [2] I take inspiration from this principle but use it differently in my Speckle Method.

In my work, I call these tiny bits *speckles*. A speckle is safe and tiny–small enough to fit on your fingertip while you're sampling food at the bench.

Children can be invited to help prepare speckles–slicing, breaking, or selecting tiny pieces as part of everyday food preparation. This can take just a few minutes at the bench before a meal is served, keeping the moment playful and natural. Parents can model curiosity by casually saying, 'I wonder if this chicken needs a little more salt,' or 'Let me taste this speckle. I want to see if it's crunchy.'

By keeping speckles tiny and pressure-free, children gradually learn that food is safe to explore, not because they are told to, but because they discover it for themselves. They may choose to imitate you tasting a speckle, or simply watch. Both are part of the learning.

Goal 2: Build problem-solving skills and flexibility with food

We all encounter small food challenges: trimming fat off meat, removing an unwanted anchovy, or managing a strong smell or texture. Most adults adjust effortlessly, but for children these moments can trigger a threat response and complete rejection.

Teaching children simple problem-solving skills around food helps them become more flexible. Instead of seeing food as all or nothing, they learn to make small adjustments–removing an ingredient, managing textures, or handling strong smells without becoming overwhelmed.

Although this practice takes place at the bench and draws on the Language of Problem-Solving from Reboot 4, it helps children carry these skills into new contexts. Flexibility at home makes it easier to navigate meals in restaurants, at school, or with extended family–settings where avoidance once felt like the only option.

Learning from adults: Katie, a neurodivergent twenty-seven-year-old, can eat salmon at a restaurant but struggles when it is served with the skin on. As a child, she could have been shown how to remove the skin herself, learning to solve the problem in the same quiet way adults set aside food they do not want.

Problem-solving visual mixed foods

Children can learn to remove offending foods, such as peas from pasta or mushrooms from pizza. Encourage them to layer foods so it can be easily separated, gradually mix ingredients to build familiarity and comfort.

> Mum Tjana is bored of eating the same limited foods that her five-year-old son accepts. Teddy only eats plain pasta. Together, we embark on a journey of gradual familiarisation with prawns and mushrooms layered onto pasta dishes. We create a safe space at the bench, where Teddy can express his comfort level and provide cues on what he can manage.
>
> When the dish is served with a small topping of mushrooms, Teddy approaches it calmly. Armed with serving tongs, he skilfully plates the plain pasta.
>
> From now on, most pasta dishes will be served with some kind of topping. With practice, small speckles of mushrooms or prawns will become familiar, and Teddy will eventually eat them without fuss.

Problem-solving chunky or mixed textures

Complex textures, especially mixed or uneven ones, often require more exposure time. Some children instinctively avoid chewing chunky foods, one child describing them as 'big fat tomato chunks, that's the problem!'

> Charlie is an eight-year-old boy on the autism spectrum. He recently sent me a picture of his taco filled to the

brim with 'the lot'. When we met two years ago, he would not even have considered mixing any food together. Since then, he has continued to hone his Food Familiarisation skills.

His mum Fiona lets me know what happened overnight when they cooked lasagna together. It was his first time making it and he expressed his displeasure when he realised the tin of crushed tomatoes would go into the mix. 'I'm not eating that,' he said firmly.

Fiona used the language of empathy, then, before she could start on the language of problem-solving, discussed in Reboot 4, he stated, 'I'm going to blend it!' That's what he did and, once cooked, he happily ate his lasagna.

This explains why a child might reject a dish like Spaghetti Bolognese—not because they dislike the flavour, but because the texture feels unpredictable and overwhelming.

Teach children to manage chunky or mixed textures by blending, mashing, or separating components. For example, they can blend vegetables into a smooth soup or mash potatoes to a preferred consistency.

Children can also experiment with food shapes and sizes by dicing foods into small cubes so they are easier to chew or place between the back teeth. This is especially helpful for children who are still developing confidence with chewing.

Tom is with his mum at a friend's place. The six-year-old quietly signals his dinner unease to his mother, who then uses the language of problem-solving to guides him:

'I can't eat this, Mum,' he says. 'I see. It looks like a difficult dish for you.' 'Yes, Mum. I can't eat the tomato bits.' 'Sounds like the chunks are the problem. Since they are in this dish, I wonder ...' 'Can you help me remove them, Mum?' 'Sure, I can. Let me grab an extra fork.'

Tom then sits happily and eats his meal next to his thrilled mum.

Problem-solving olfactory challenges

Some smells arrive suddenly, such as when food is reheated or unwrapped. For children with smell sensitivities, this can feel overwhelming and trigger distress or avoidance.

Strong smells do not have to be endured as they are. They can be dispersed or balanced with another scent. When children understand that smells can be changed rather than simply tolerated, they feel less trapped and more in control.

Simple adjustments can help reduce intensity. Opening a window, using a fan, or stepping briefly out of the room gives children a way to manage strong smells themselves. Being involved in cooking or food preparation can also help, as it allows aromas to build gradually rather than arriving all at once.

Pairing a strong smell with a preferred scent, such as lighting a candle, can further support regulation.

Once five-year-old Agatha learned to ask her mum to light a candle during Food Familiarisation activities, her smell-related meltdowns stopped. The candle helped her feel calmer. What was striking was that, once Agatha felt in control of how she responded to smells, her sensitivity reduced to the point where she no longer needed the candle at all.

Problem-solving gustatory challenges

Children naturally problem-solve taste by masking strong flavours with tomato sauce or cheese. Encouraging this instinct while making seasonings accessible–within reason–helps them learn to adjust flavours on their own.

Introducing new flavours gradually helps children adapt without feeling overwhelmed. Pairing unfamiliar tastes with familiar foods–

like mixing a small amount of tomato paste with butter or olive oil in pasta–can ease the transition.

> Will's mum would love him to learn to eat tomato sauce with his pasta and maybe one day, pasta Bolognese. Using a brush, Will paints the pasta with tomato paste (1/4 of a teaspoon initially, mixed with butter and olive oil). Will refuses to eat the pasta. The next time, he doesn't want to help prepare the pasta, however his mum follows the same recipe. At dinner, Will hesitates, then eats the pasta and decides he loves it.
>
> Using the same technique, six-year-old Sofia overcomes her difficulty and eats slightly coloured pasta. Within three weeks, she is back to eating spaghetti Bolognese, a dish she hasn't eaten in years.

Goal 3: Build Confidence Through Food Skills

Cooking is more than a life skill–it's a gateway to food confidence. For extreme fussy eaters, preparing food reduces anxiety and makes eating feel less intimidating. The act of handling, modifying, and presenting food helps children feel capable and in control.

In my hypnotherapy work with adults who have lived with life-long extreme fussy eating, a consistent pattern emerges: their practical food skills are often very limited. Many never learned how to handle, prepare, or modify foods, so their sensory sensitivities stayed the same for years–leaving them with little confidence and few tools for managing challenging foods. This is why building food skills early matters so much; it protects children from carrying unnecessary fear and avoidance into adulthood.

Learning from adults: Take Charles, for example. As a child, he could have gained confidence through simple skills like peeling, squeezing, or cutting an orange. He might have used oranges to bake a cake, make salad dressing, or prepare fresh juice for the family. Along the way, he would have learned to deal with sticky fingers and strong smells–helping him grow more comfortable with the fruit. If he'd had these experiences early on, tackling oranges might not have felt so daunting as an adult.

Charles, thirty-four, sits down to talk about a food he finally feels ready to try.

'I want to give oranges a go,' he admits, 'but I have no idea where to start. I just picture it as this sticky, gooey mess with peels everywhere! I can't ask my foodie girlfriend, I'd be too embarrassed.'

Children who actively participate in food preparation learn to adjust textures, balance flavours, and manage sensory challenges. They discover that the same ingredient can taste, feel, and look completely different depending on how it's prepared–helping them become more flexible eaters.

Research consistently shows that food skills, not nutrition knowledge, predict a more varied and balanced diet. Confidence in practical skills such as chopping, seasoning, adjusting textures, and combining flavours naturally leads people to enjoy a wider range of foods. In other words, cooking ability rather than nutritional theory supports lifelong healthy eating.[3,4]

Gustatory improvement

Research by Professor Carolyn Ross has shown that pairing flavours can help texture-sensitive children accept new foods.[5]

Pairing uses complementary flavours to balance or soften challenging tastes and textures, making foods feel more approachable. For example, adding a touch of sweetness can reduce bitterness in vegetables. Umami ingredients such as cheese or soy sauce can deepen savoury notes and soften sharp edges. These combinations help children engage with foods that might otherwise feel too strong or unpleasant.

How food is prepared can significantly change how it tastes and feels in the mouth. Cooking methods such as roasting, baking, or pan-frying bring out natural sweetness through browning and caramelisation, while boiling or steaming may preserve more bitter or sharp notes. These changes can enhance flavour pairing without altering the food itself.

Teaching children to adjust flavour builds skill and confidence. Umami boosters such as cheese, soy sauce, Vegemite, teriyaki, or bacon can enhance savoury dishes. Sweet elements like honey, caramel, or vanilla can help balance bitter or sour tastes. Nutty notes introduced through roasting or nut butters add depth, warmth, and texture.

When children learn that flavour can be adjusted rather than endured, food becomes something they can work with. This sense of agency supports curiosity and long-term acceptance.

Appearance and presentation empowerment

Let children have a go at shaping and presenting food with cookie cutters, moulds, or safety knives. I've seen how a simple change in shape—cutting fruit into a heart or moulding rice into a triangle—can make all the difference. I've watched kids turn down loose rice but happily eat it once it's shaped, and enjoy fruit for the first time, all because of these small, playful touches.

6yo with ASD, rigid about food presentation, tries hard boiled egg for the first time as he prepared it himself.

Take the picture above: had the hard-boiled eggs simply been served, the child would have refused them on sight. But by being involved in the process and presentation, he felt a sense of control, which led to spontaneous tasting and, eventually, eating them at dinner.

Texture improvement

Children can learn to coat foods in crumbs, batter, or tempura–testing it out with all sorts, from meat and fish to vegetables. Sometimes, just cooking something a bit longer is enough to get that lovely crunch. Children can also make crispy toppings–like breadcrumbs or cheese–for pasta bakes, mashed potatoes, or even a proper gratin, giving dishes that golden, crunchy finish.

As they gain confidence using a food processor, they may enjoy creating silky soups, smooth sauces, or creamy mashed vegetables. This gives them control over texture and shows how cooking skills can turn simple foods into something both comfortable and delicious.

> At eleven years old, Flynn, who is on the autism spectrum, struggles when mashed potatoes don't turn out exactly how he likes them. His mum knows that if the texture isn't right, it can lead to a meltdown.
>
> So, once Flynn learns the skills, he takes charge of making sure the mashed potatoes are just how he likes them. Giving him this control not only empowers him but also helps prevent difficult reactions.

HOW TO GET STARTED

Pick a consistent time

Set aside dedicated time each week for Food Familiarisation–away from mealtimes. Even a few minutes can make a difference. A clear heads-up helps the transition feel planned rather than a sudden interruption of screen time.

Sofia's father decided he would be the one taking charge of familiarisation activities. He can only do so once a week, but as long as he keeps it as regular as possible, that is all that's needed.

He alternates between two different activities on Saturday mornings–taking eight-year-old Sofia to the market or making brunch together.

Best places for Food Familiarisation

- The shop, market, or garden: a relaxed setting where children can explore food, knowing there is no expectation to eat.
- The kitchen bench: a hands-on space where they can naturally engage with food.
- Other options: if your dining table doubles as a prep space or the backyard feels right, use what works!

Jack now loves supermarket trips, especially when the lights are dimmed, and the music is quieter. His mum asks him to pick out mushrooms or tomatoes, and at seven, his curiosity is growing. He's also becoming much more comfortable handling different textures and smells in food.

Create a safe workstation

The key elements required for a safe and child-friendly workstation are:

- a learning tower or sturdy stool that lets children safely stand at the bench
- a chopping board and child-safe knife
- fun tools like vegetable peelers or sandwich cutters
- a tea towel or apron so they can wipe their hands without stress

Make it fun!

A joyful, playful approach makes Food Familiarisation engaging. Prioritise laughter, but always make sure it lands on you, not your child.

Parents can put themselves on the receiving end of the silliness: a dab of flour on your nose, pretending spaghetti is a moustache, letting a carrot 'bonk' you on the head. When the fun is directed at you, your child feels safe, and free to simply watch.

Seven-year-old Alexandra has autism and is cautious about the food she will accept. Her mother Julie accepts my playful challenge, agreeing to be blindfolded to guess what garden herbs I brought. Alexandra's job is to crush one herb in her hand so Julie can smell it. Then she offers the herb to Julie to taste. Laughter erupts in the room. As soon as Julie is done, Alexandra jumps in and says, 'I want to have a go.' Alexandra's inner motivation has surfaced. We have not asked her to taste the herbs; she did it of her own accord.

When children are ready, they usually join in–not because they were invited or asked, but because the atmosphere feels warm, relaxed, and genuinely playful.

Six-year old Zoe is on the autism spectrum. She used to eat peas when she was eighteen months old. Preparing dinner, we are learning to cook peas in the microwave. As we put the frozen peas on the bench, Zoe's father walks past, and I ask if he can catch a pea in his mouth. After a few trials, he succeeds, and Zoe thinks it's hilarious. I then say, 'I will show you my special trick!'

We go out to the garden. I take one pea out of the bag, put it in my mouth and spit it out as far as I can. Before I know it, Zoe is playing too. Within seconds, she is munching and swallowing frozen peas. We go back to the kitchen, and I leave the bag out in case Zoe wants more peas as we cook. She does.

Later, that night, I receive a message: Zoe ate cooked peas!

I am not a huge advocate for playing with foods. However simple sensory play can help very young children explore textures in a relaxed way–things like toy cars driving through jelly or dinosaurs 'hiding' in food. For little ones who enjoy this kind of play, it can gently support familiarity without any pressure.

Olivia could see three-year-old Will was struggling with touching gooey, sticky textures. We combined short activities at the bench during food prep, and some play activities during the day.

Will would run away from banana but recently took great pleasure mashing one into a pulp at the bench. As he did, he was exposed to the change of texture and the smell. He remained calm all along.

Olivia also keeps a tray of jelly in the fridge. She brings it outside and Will has fun running his toys through it. He can now put his hand through the jelly very comfortably.

Let your child's cues guide the pace, not the plan

Pay attention to your child's cues–they'll show you how they're coping. If they're struggling with a food or activity, you'll notice. Some children react strongly to smells, while others find touching textures tricky.

The key is to help them build skills to handle specific, challenging foods, while ensuring they feel regulated and supported during Food Familiarisation. The foods are chosen deliberately; your child's cues simply guide how quickly you move.

Fred has a new job as 'cheese master'. At dinner, every night, the four-year-old places grated cheese in a colourful cup and brings it to the dinner table. Fred now comfortably eats cheddar, mozzarella and parmesan.

Rolling chicken in egg mix would have been unthinkable 1 year ago for this 5.5 yo autistic boy

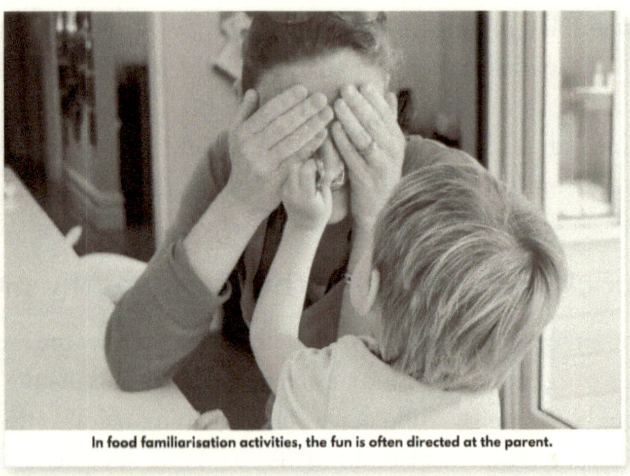

In food familiarisation activities, the fun is often directed at the parent.

CHOOSE SPECIFIC FOODS FOR FAMILIARISATION

Any food your child refuses to eat can be a focus for Food Familiarisation. Once you've identified the most important foods for your family to work with, you can use the three goals as a framework. At the end of the activity, as introduced in Goal 1, always taste the speckles and bring any spares to the dinner table with the rest of the food.

Fruit

1. If your child refuses banana, begin with simple preparation tasks such as peeling and cutting it. Sensory engagement begins naturally without any pressure to eat.
2. Next show them how to remove the black spots or fibrous strings, an important problem-solving skill that reduces overwhelm.
3. Then move into simple cooking together, helping make bananas potentially more palatable, such as a quick banana sorbet, adding banana to pancakes, or baking a banana cake.

Step by step, your child becomes familiar with banana in different forms, gains practical skills that make more approachable.

Vegetables

1. If your child refuses vegetables, begin with simple preparation tasks. Peas, corn, or spinach work well because preparation may be as simple as scooping them from a bag into a cup. This creates natural sensory engagement without pressure. Be playful and see if your child follows your lead: pouring peas into a bowl, transferring corn with a spoon, or 'catching' spinach leaves with tongs.
2. Next, build problem-solving skills by mixing these vegetables into rice or pasta and showing how they can be added, then removed at the bench. This gives your child a chance to practise problem-solving before the mixed dish appears at the dinner table.
3. Then together explore ways to make vegetables more appealing through cooking: crispy peas, golden mini quiches

with greens, or adding cheese for extra flavour. These small variations show your child that vegetables can change texture and taste, and become much more approachable.

Protein

Meat

1. If your child refuses meat, begin with forms that are easier to chew. Meat has a firmer texture and requires more mature chewing, which can feel overwhelming for texture-sensitive children. Start with minced meat. Children can help make mini kebabs by mixing mince with bread soaked in milk or egg to create a softer texture. This provides natural sensory engagement through mixing, shaping, and threading the meat onto small sticks. Steak and other meats can still be offered as thin strips or small pieces. Children might place toothpicks in the pieces before serving, giving them a sense of control over how they handle the food.

2. Next comes problem solving. If your child is sensitive to certain smells, such as pork or lamb, show them how to switch on the exhaust fan or light a candle to soften the scent in the room. If flavour seems to be the challenge, invite them to add a little butter or olive oil, or prepare a small ramekin of sauce. This reinforces the idea that foods can be adjusted in ways that feel safe. Of course we are also looking at them separating the meat from a liked dish, if they are not ready to have it yet.

3. From there, explore the many ways meat can be prepared, slow cooked in a stew, softened in a casserole, or grilled and sliced thinly. Marinades can also transform flavour and tenderness. As children learn to navigate these variations, meat becomes less daunting and more familiar.

Eggs

1. If your child refuses eggs, begin with simple preparation tasks. Children can slice, quarter, or mash hard-boiled eggs before serving. This offers natural sensory engagement as they handle the smooth white, the crumbly yolk, and the egg smell, all without any pressure to eat.
2. Next comes problem-solving: if your child currently prefers egg whites, teach them how to remove the yolk themselves. This builds confidence and shows them they can manage foods in ways that feel safe. Smells can also be managed as discussed in the meat section above.
3. From there, explore the many ways eggs can be cooked–boiled, scrambled, fried, or turned into omelette strips. Each method changes the texture, colour, and flavour. You might show your child how to spread a thin layer of scrambled egg onto crunchy bread or cut an omelette into fun shapes. As children learn to control these variations, eggs feel less threatening and more interesting.

Dairy

1. If your child isn't yet ready to eat yoghurt, invite them to interact with it in simple, pressure-free ways. They can spoon yoghurt into a small serving cup and mix it with honey, before bringing it to the dinner table for the family to share.
2. Next, if yoghurt with fruit is too challenging, teach them how to retrieve the 'offending bits' into a side bowl. This small problem-solving skill helps reduce overwhelm and increases confidence. If yoghurt tastes too sour, let your child learn how to sweeten it by mixing in honey, maple syrup, or a little fruit coulis.
3. Frozen yoghurt, either store-bought or homemade, can feel more approachable than the cold, wobbly texture of fresh

yoghurt. Together, you can create a yoghurt bar with toppings your child enjoys sprinkling on, or make yoghurt parfaits or yoghurt cake.

Carbohydrates

1. If your child refuses rice, begin by involving them in simple, low-pressure tasks. They can scoop dry rice into cups or containers–a calming sensory experience. Once the cooked rice has cooled, invite them to press it into onigiri moulds or shape small rice balls with damp hands. These activities help your child manage texture and stickiness–all while building confidence and familiarity with rice in different forms.

2. Next, invite your child to place rice alongside a liked food, such as sausage, on a serving dish. This allows them to keep foods separate before they feel comfortable layering food on top of the rice. When they're ready, you can move to gentle mixing. For example your child can add sliced sausage to the rice and practice removing it at the bench.

3. As children grow more familiar, explore cooking together: make mini arancini, mix rice with a little cheese, or create crispy rice patties in a pan. Show your child risottos and fried rice if they're part of your family repertoire.

Condiments, sauces, marinades, dips

1. If your child avoids tomato-based sauces, begin by letting them prepare small ramekins with different types of tomato sauce. Later, show them how a tiny amount of tomato paste can "disappear" when blended with butter or olive oil. Once loosened, it melts smoothly into pasta or spreads easily onto bread, becoming barely noticeable. When young children feel they have made it disappear, they often cope much better with its presence. Together increase quantity over time.

2. Then support your child to practise problem-solving, such as removing tomato chunks, mashing them with a fork, or blending the sauce until smooth. Step by step, your child discovers that tomato or vegetables chunks in sauce can be managed, adjusted, and transformed, making more manageable.

3. Together, explore simple sauces or marinades, experimenting with flavours, textures, and colours.

THE PROCESSING BUFFER

Food Familiarisation activities can vary in length, but they all give children a moment to process what is being served. When time is short, even showing your child what you are preparing or letting them carry food to the table can help. The Speckles Method described in Chapter 15 is particularly useful on busy days.

This Processing Buffer allows your child to express any worries about the meal. For example, they might complain when they see a mixed dish being made. But by giving them space to voice their concerns ahead of time, they can mentally prepare for what's coming.

When children complain at the bench rather than the table, it gives parents the chance to use the language of empathy and problem-solving ahead of time. Once their worries have been acknowledged and addressed–see Reboot 4–mealtime itself can be calm and complaint-free.

Parents notice the shift when the child's shoulders drop, their face relaxes, and the moment feels less charged.

The goal is to create a happy, relaxed atmosphere by the time the child sits at the table. In effect, it becomes a no-complaint zone, but you and your child can give it a more positive name, perhaps a 'joyful table' or something that feels right for your family.

DEEPENING RELAXATION

By now, mealtimes likely feel more natural. You have stepped back from pressure, established routines, and begun sharing power. The atmosphere is calmer.

Food Familiarisation builds three core capacities: sensory exposure that reduces fear, problem solving skills, and ways to make food more palatable. Once established, these skills do not disappear. They quietly support your child at the table day after day.

Deepening relaxation is about building trust in yourself, in your child, and in the process. Your child learns that meals are safe and predictable. You learn that stepping back does not mean losing control but creating the conditions for learning.

At this stage, your child's nervous system settles more quickly at mealtimes. Fight, flight, or freeze responses ease, and curiosity becomes more available. This is where the work begins to show. A child separates foods, removes a piece, adjusts texture, tolerates smells, or adds flavour on their own accord.

To support this stage, keep reinforcing calm predictability:

- Stick with your routines: the same rhythm of when, where, and how food is served.
- Hold firm to the Division of Responsibility: you provide, your child decides.
- Make Food Familiarisation activities predictable so your child knows when to expect them.

The deeper this sense of safety becomes, the more energy your child has for exploration. For you, relaxation comes from seeing progress without having to push. Mealtimes shift from effortful to steady, creating the conditions for the next phase of change.

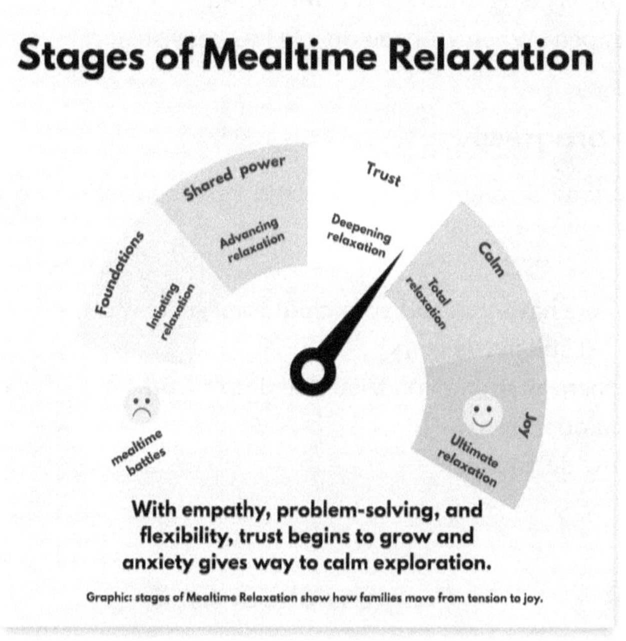

With empathy, problem-solving, and flexibility, trust begins to grow and anxiety gives way to calm exploration.

Graphic: stages of Mealtime Relaxation show how families move from tension to joy.

REBOOT 3: LET'S GO!

Observe

- Is your child wary of being messy and becoming tactile with food?
- Are you quick to react and clean them up?

Take action

1. Do you need a play activity for a toddler or is cooking feasible?
2. Is your child secure at the bench, and using a step or a learning tower?
3. How often will you take your child shopping? How often will you have your child at the bench?

4. Who is going to do Food Familiarisation? Where will it happen? When will you do it? How consistent can you be?

Assess progress

After working through Reboot 3, stand back and reflect on what has changed.

- Where have you and your child been successful?
- What still needs work?
- Is there anything you tried that didn't work–and what can you do instead?
- How do you feel?

Reboot

3

Progress Check-list 3

Parents understand 3 goals of food exploration ☐

Parents Decide when, where and what of Food Familiarisation ☐

Safe workstation station ready ☐

Parents nail no pressure, fun Food Familiarisation ☐

Parents nail the Speckle Method and the Processing Buffer ☐

From refusal to familiarity

REBOOT 4–WHAT YOU SAY MATTERS MORE THAN YOU THINK

So far, you've put strong foundations in place. Through the first three Reboots, you've created structure, reduced pressure, and begun tackling food in ways that support safety rather than struggle.

Now, the focus shifts to language. In this Reboot, you'll learn how to use words deliberately and calmly to reinforce everything you've already built. This shared language brings together structure, empathy, problem-solving, flexibility, and Food Familiarisation, helping your child understand what's happening and what's expected without increasing pressure.

By the end of this Reboot, you will:

- analyse your language, moving away from language that enables your child's fussy eating
- choose language that supports both you and your child
- practise using your shared language together consistently

UNHELPFUL LANGUAGE AND ACTIONS

As parents, we can slip into being *dismissive, reinforcing, pressurising, or negatively labelling* in the way we speak and act around food. None of these patterns works.

As you've seen earlier, they only fuel avoidance–often a product of your child's threat response.

- **Dismissive**: 'Come on, it's only cheese, don't be silly.'
- **Reinforcing**: 'I didn't add cheese because you don't like it.'
- **Pressurising**: 'Just one more bite and then dessert.'
- **Negative labelling**: 'She's such a fussy eater.'

Each of these responses may feel small in the moment, but together they create more tension, less trust, and more avoidance.

This is why we now turn to building a shared language–words and actions that validate feelings, maintain structure, and reduce pressure, giving your child the security to explore food at their own pace.

BUILD YOUR SHARED LANGUAGE TOWARDS RESILIENCE

The next step is to move beyond language like 'You don't have to eat it if you don't like it'–away from the black-and-white of liking versus not liking food.

The goal is to move children away from the idea of 'my food' versus 'Mum and Dad's food', and instead towards understanding all food as family food.

Building a shared language of structure, empathy, problem-solving, flexibility, mealtime, rebranding, positive mindset, and food exploration provides the pillars for developing a resilient eater.

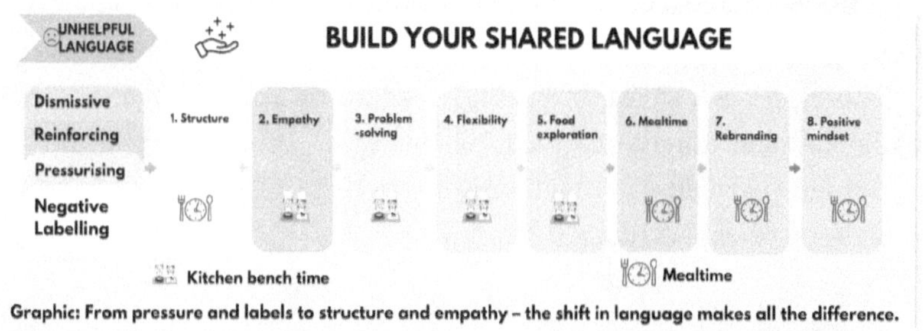

Graphic: From pressure and labels to structure and empathy – the shift in language makes all the difference.

Language of structure

From the very first Reboot, structure has been central. Clear, consistent language reduces uncertainty, clarifies expectations, and helps a child's nervous system stay regulated during transitions.

Now and then

As discussed in Reboot 1, children benefit from transitions using the 'now and then' structure:

- 'Now you wash your hands, then the kitchen is open.'
- 'Now you sit properly, then you help yourself to dinner.'
- 'Now the kitchen is closed, then you take your plate to the sink.'
- 'Now you play and then, in 15 minutes, we will prepare lunch together.'

Double bind

If you interrupt a favourite activity and ask your child, 'Would you like to help me…?', the answer will almost certainly be no. Children need planning and notice.

However, to foster your child's participation in activities, such as food exposure, you can use a technique known as 'double binds'.

A double bind presents your child with two choices, both of which are acceptable to you. For example, you might ask, 'Would you like to rinse the rice or crack the egg?' or 'Would you like to put some mushrooms in this bag or pick some bananas?'

This approach gives your child a sense of autonomy and control while keeping them involved in the task. It is a subtle way to encourage participation without overwhelming them with direct commands or expectations.

1–2–3 Magic

The 1–2–3 Magic approach, developed by American psychologist Dr T. Phelan and introduced in Australia by Michael Hawton, encourages parents to talk less, listen more, and guide children with quiet authority which supports calm, connected mealtimes.[1, 2]

You calmly count from 1 to 3, leaving a 5–10 second gap between each number. This short pause gives children, especially those under seven, time to shift gears and respond without conflict.

The aim isn't punishment but calm consistency. Counting sets clear boundaries, prevents spirals into arguments, and helps children feel safe within limits while keeping the parent–child connection intact.

Language of empathy and validation

As we saw in Reboot 2, even praise can slip into pressure. What helps more is empathy, shifting the focus away from eating or liking the food and toward readiness. Saying *'It sounds like you're not ready yet'* leaves the door open for progress without pushing.

Dr Thomas Gordon introduced active listening to parenting, and it remains one of the most effective tools here.[3] Sandra Blackard, in her book *Say What You See*, also shows how describing what you notice helps children feel understood. This reduces anxiety and makes them feel safe enough to stay engaged with food.[4]

These conversations belong at the bench or in the shop, not at the dinner table. Problem-solving and buffering before meals are where children can begin processing what to do with food, as discussed in Reboot 3.

Stage 1–Describe what you see or hear

At the bench or shop, state what you notice, without judgement.

- 'I hear that you are unhappy about what I've cooked.'
- 'I can see you're pinching your nose.'
- 'I hear you don't want to eat this.'
- 'I can see you poked your tongue out, looking at this dish.'
- 'I can see you're not ready to crack the egg by yourself quite yet.'

Stage 2–State the obvious

Give calm, matter-of-fact reminders about the food or the rules.

- 'It's my job to decide what I serve for dinner, but there is always something you can eat at the table!'
- 'Eggs can get a bit messy and sticky.'
- 'You see I cooked this dish because that's what I want to serve to our family.'
- 'That's what the recipe calls for.'

Once your child feels understood, you can gently guide them to finding their own solutions. That's where the language of problem-solving comes in.

Stage 3–Problem-solve

This final stage is about initiating problem-solving and building some resilience around food.

Language of problem-solving

Problem-solving language invites children to think for themselves. Instead of rushing in with answers, you help them come up with their own strategies. This builds resilience and turns food into something they can manage, not fear.

Examples might sound like this:

- 'You know what? We always have something you can eat on the table. I wonder…What do you think you'll eat first?'
- 'When there's a smell that bothers you, you're always welcome to tell me. Now let's see what ideas you have to make it easier for you.'
- 'That's right, you can eat bread, yoghurt and fruit. See? You worked it out.'
- 'It's a great idea to use your special tongs to help yourself around the sauce.'
- 'You'll remove the peas and put them in the side bowl? That sounds like a good idea.'
- 'You can work it out.'

Problem-solving takes practice. Each time your child finds their own solution, they build confidence, resilience, and trust in their abilities.

Remember: mealtimes are not the place for these discussions. If your child starts to complain, remind them of the solutions they already worked out with you at the bench:

- 'Remember we talked about this at the bench, and you came up with a great idea? You can work it out. Now let's enjoy our lunch and then, this afternoon, we're going to the park.'
- 'Remember our dinner rule is to be polite. You came up with a great idea earlier on. You can work it out.'

Language of flexibility

If rigidity and flexibility pull in opposite directions, where does your child tend to settle, and when does rigidity show up most? Many sensitive children use rigidity to manage anxiety, food surprises can feel overwhelming. Supporting flexibility helps them cope with change, both around food and beyond the table.

As Jed Baker, author of *No More Meltdowns*, shows, rehearsing changes in advance helps worried children adapt more easily.[5]

Knowing what *changes* and what *stays the same* reduces stress and increases confidence.

Practising food-related changes at the shop or the bench builds readiness before mealtime. For example:

- 'What changes?'–'The pasta is a different shape'.
- 'What stays the same?'–'It's still pasta, with the same sauce'.

Flexibility also helps in social situations, like cafés, school camps, or eating at a friend's house. Preparing in advance gives your child more confidence to enjoy food and the experience around it.

Priya, aged ten, was nervous about going to an Indian restaurant for her grandfather's birthday. The day before, she told her mum:

'I don't know what I'll be able to eat.' Her mum reassured her by rehearsing flexibility:

'What changes? The chef makes their own naan bread.' Then, *'and what stays the same?* It's still naan bread and rice, just like at home.'

With this reminder, Priya felt calmer. On the day, she rehearsed a few options on the way to the restaurant. She arrived more relaxed, joined in, and enjoyed the meal with her family.

Language of food exploration

After building safety through structure, empathy, and problem-solving, you can bring curiosity into food. Food exploration is not about asking children to taste or try. As discussed earlier, that adds pressure. Instead, it's about parents modelling curiosity out loud.

You might simply wonder aloud at the bench or shop: *'This cheese smells a bit sharp today'* or *'These crackers look extra crunchy'*. You're not asking your child to respond; you're modelling how to notice. By thinking out loud rather than speaking directly to the child, parents model curiosity and openness. This invites children to explore food with their senses, without judgement or pressure.

Over time, this gentle narration helps children feel less anxious and more open, because they are free to observe without expectation.

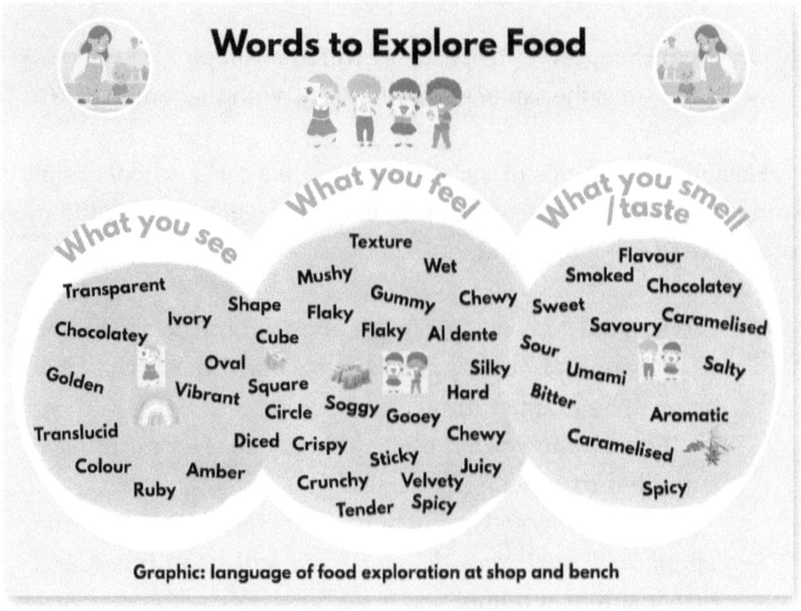

Graphic: language of food exploration at shop and bench

Language of mealtime

Once you and your child have stepped away from talking about food or eating at the table, mealtimes open up as a space for connection and conversation that supports your child's development and wellbeing.

These conversations work best as a gentle back-and-forth, with parents setting the rhythm while staying responsive to their child's cues. Open-ended questions invite engagement far more effectively than closed ones like 'Was school fun today?'

For example:

- 'Tell me about something that made you laugh today.'
- 'What was the best part of playtime?'

In his research on resilience, discussed in Reboot 1, Marshall Duke identified a set of simple questions that reflect how well children know their family stories. Children who grow up hearing these shared narratives tend to feel a stronger sense of belonging and cope more effectively with stress.

Examples include:

- 'Do you know where grandpa and grandma grew up?'
- 'Do you know how mum and dad met?'
- 'Do you know about a time when someone in our family faced a challenge and got through it?'

Some families also use a 'talking stick' or shared object to signal turns–a shell, a pepper mill, or a spoon–sitting in the middle of the table and hopping from hand to hand as the conversation unfolds. This simple practice supports patience, listening, and respect, while ensuring every voice has space to be heard.

At times, it also helps to let adult conversation flow naturally, giving children space rather than placing the focus on them. When the spotlight softens, many children relax, explore their food quietly, or even try something new on their own.

Language of rebranding

The way we speak about our children, and how others do too, quietly shapes how they see themselves. A child's self-talk, such as 'I'm the weirdest kid at school; I don't eat like everyone else', can come from many places, including the words used to describe them. Words matter. Offhand comments can reinforce the idea of being a 'fussy eater', or they can gently steer children towards seeing themselves as learners, explorers, or budding chefs.

When dinner becomes tense, it is easy to fall into shorthand labels. But focusing too much on a child's eating, even with concern, can backfire. Instead, we can begin to reframe how they see themselves: not as a 'problem eater', but as someone who is learning. A future cook. A creative food adventurer.

So what might we call these kids now? How about:

- a learner eater
- a curious explorer
- a budding chef
- a future foodie
- a cheese master

Rebranding does not ignore a child's struggles; it reframes them as part of their learning journey.

Rebranding in action

I remember one dinner clearly. A friend arrived with her daughter and, with a laugh, said, 'You'll be lucky if she eats this, she's such a fussy eater!' That one remark landed straight in the child's ears. She looked dismissed, even embarrassed. I was too. The comment cut off the quiet space she needed to explore food at her own pace.

It's easy to fall back on labels. But highlighting a child's eating, even with concern, can reinforce the 'fussy eater' identity.

As you remove pressure, spoken and unspoken, your child may wonder: where's the attention gone? What happened to the special treatment? Why isn't anyone watching my plate anymore? They will notice the change and they will adjust to their new status.

Jamie shared that during a pleasant phone call, her sister Kate unexpectedly interjected, asking, 'Is Abbey still on crackers?' This jarring moment made Jamie acutely aware of her family's perception of her child's eating habits.

Consequently, Jamie has been diligently working to shift this perception. She now occasionally drops comments, such as 'Abbey is developing into quite the chef' and 'she is learning so much and loves to help me with grocery shopping.'

Helping children notice their progress

Part of rebranding is helping children see their own growth. Not through vague praise like 'Good boy' or 'Good girl', but with observations that reflect real effort, curiosity or change:

- 'You're enjoying it more, aren't you?'
- 'It's getting easier with practice, isn't it?'
- 'You're becoming more curious every day. Aren't you?'
- 'I wonder what's changing today that wasn't there before?'
- 'You may surprise yourself.'
- 'You surprised yourself, didn't you?'

These gentle reflections foster self-awareness, not just self-esteem. They allow children to notice their progress for themselves–anchoring a stronger, more confident identity around food.

Language of a positive mindset

The words you tell yourself shape the tone of mealtimes. A calm, positive mindset in you creates trust and ease in your child. This further supports co-regulation: your state helps theirs.

> Charleen's daughter spat out beans, but Charleen tells me she felt fine, she saw progress, not dislike.

This kind of reframing shifts the focus from outcome to effort. Progress is not defined by swallowing a food, but by the steps taken towards it.

Earlier in the book, you were asked to reflect on emotions. This is where that work pays off. Calm is contagious. Language can help you get further. Using simple affirmations before meals can support a calmer mindset:

- 'I trust my child's innate ability to learn to eat.'
- 'My child knows when they are hungry and when they are full.'
- 'I am doing my job by providing nourishing options. My child decides how much to eat.'

Graphic: A positive Mindset allows for positive co-regulation

This completes the fourth Reboot: language becomes not just a tool for regulating, but a foundation for trust and resilience. It is now precise and effective.

TOTAL RELAXATION

At this point, calm has become your family's default mealtime setting. Total relaxation means mealtimes feel predictable and safe for everyone. Your child knows there will always be something they can eat, so anxiety is low. Your child's mealtime meltdowns are a thing of the past.

In this stage, the benefits ripple outwards:

- siblings relax too, enjoying mealtimes without disruption
- parents rediscover the pleasure of eating together, not just monitoring plates

- the whole family experiences less stress, more laughter, and more presence at the table

Notice how your child's confidence grows here. They are starting to take the lead–exploring new foods, tolerating variety, or simply enjoying the comfort of staples.

The shared language you've built, the routines you've set, and the power you've balanced all converge here. What was once a battlefield now feels like a refuge.

Take a deep breath. You've created a calm foundation your child can keep building on.

Graphic: stages of Mealtime Relaxation show how families move from tension to joy.

REBOOT 4: LET'S GO!

Observe

- What language do you usually use around food?
- How does your child react to the language used?

- Are there any behaviours that are not acceptable, such as climbing on the table during meals. Would these behaviours benefit from being managed with 1–2–3 magic?
- What does your mindset tell you as you endeavour to feed your child?

Take action

1. Choose your language of structure.
2. Choose your language of positive mindset.
3. Practise your language of empathy and problem-solving away from the dinner table.
4. Take cues from your child at the bench. As you see discomfort, or they express it, initiate language of problem-solving.
5. Nip dinnertime complaints straight away and redirect conversation away from food.
6. Rebrand your child as a learner eater or little chef in the making.

Assess progress

After working through Reboot 4, stand back and reflect on what has changed.

- Where have you and your child been successful?
- What still needs work?
- Is there anything you tried that didn't work–and what can you do instead?
- How do you feel?

Reboot

Progress Check-list 4

Parents use language of empathy and validation ☐

Parents use language of problem-solving ☐

Child initiates some problem-solving around food ☐

Mealtime conversations are friendly, no-complaint dinnertime ☐

End of dinnertime meltdowns, deepening relaxation. ☐

What you say matters more than you think

CHAPTER 17

REBOOT 5–TURNING IDEAS INTO EVERYDAY MEALS

It's time to enhance your Meal System. You've already established it through mains and staples. In this Reboot, you'll take that structure into the real world of food shopping and cooking, adapting it so it works for your child and your family.

Now is the time to streamline your food choices, spot gaps, and build a repertoire that reflects your family's real-life needs, preferences, and values. It is also a chance to add in foods you have put on hold, ones that matter to you culturally, nutritionally, or simply because you love them.

By the end of this Reboot, you will have:

1. Reviewed what you usually buy and prepare, alongside new foods you're curious to introduce.
2. Identified what guides your cooking, whether specific foods, methods, or cuisines, so you reduce decision fatigue, the mental load of deciding what to cook day after day.
3. Built a structured but flexible repertoire that supports your child's learning over time.

CHOOSING FOODS THAT MATTER TO YOUR FAMILY

Children often grow up to eat like their parents–it's one of those quiet truths of family life.[1]

What you buy, cook, and enjoy shapes your child's food world. Pausing to identify the foods that matter most to your family–the comforting, cultural, and celebratory dishes you value–helps anchor your Meal System in meaning rather than pressure. Even when children aren't ready to eat these foods, repeated, low-key exposure builds familiarity. For many learner eaters, this familiarity is what eventually opens the door to acceptance.

This reflection can also reveal gaps shaped by adult habits. Perhaps one parent dislikes fish, so it rarely appears at home. Noticing these patterns allows you to decide deliberately which foods you want to keep, reintroduce, or explore again as a family.

With this clarity, expanding your repertoire becomes practical rather than overwhelming. Start with what's already in rotation, then add thoughtfully–whether that's a forgotten favourite, a new ingredient, or a dish you'd like to welcome back to the table. The aim isn't maximum variety, but a calm, predictable system that reflects your family's values and supports learning.

When food choices are intentional, decision fatigue drops. Children benefit from repeated, pressure-free exposure to foods that matter–creating the conditions for confidence and curiosity to grow over time.

It was important to me that our family ate snails at Christmas. I began to offer them when my children were little, going all out to source the snails in Australia and crafting the perfect garlic and parsley butter with a hint of Cognac. Now, it's a Christmas must for our family and friends, there's no getting out of making the snails without disappointing everyone.

CHOOSING COOKING METHODS THAT FIT YOUR WEEK

How food is cooked matters just as much as what is cooked. Cooking methods change flavour, texture, and smell, and they also shape how manageable meals feel for you.

Match methods to real life. On low-energy nights, choose minimal-cook options. When you have more time, let the oven or slow cooker do the work. The same ingredient can feel entirely different depending on the method, which is especially helpful for building flexibility.

Below, I've broken down cooking options to fit different energy levels, time frames, and goals:

Low-effort meals for low-energy days

Ideal for those evenings when you need something quick and low fuss. These meals rely on assembling, reheating, or opening foods, rather than active cooking. Think:

- sandwiches, wraps, or toasties
- cheese boards, antipasto-style platters or simple salads
- yoghurt parfaits
- store-bought sushi rolls or roast chicken
- fish and Chips or pizza
- reheated left-overs
- tinned fish or legumes

Short cook meals: 10–20 mins

Perfect for nights when you've got a little more time and energy:

- grilling or pan-frying
- steaming
- poaching
- simple stir-fries or quick sautés

Meals that cook while you get on with life

For when you've got time earlier in the day or want the oven or slow-cooker to do the work while you get on with life:

- braising
- roasting
- slow-cooking stews or casseroles

Regardless of how much time you've got, the goal is the same: to make food prep more predictable for you, and more approachable for your child. Plus, trying different cooking methods is a great way to show your learner eater how one ingredient can feel completely different depending on how it's prepared–a great tool for flexibility and food learning.

Taking the thinking out of dinner

Building a weekly rhythm can help you get started. Choose a simple frame–by cooking method, core ingredient, or cuisine–based on the time and energy you have.

Core Ingredient	Cooking Method	Cuisine
Chicken	Panfried chicken	Italian

LISTS THAT REDUCE STRESS AND REPETITION

Preparing your shopping list by category helps you shop once a week and avoid last-minute stress. Once your basics are in place, a small set of pantry staples can be turned into many different meals. There are two lists to keep visible:

- Your current list: What you reliably buy, prepare, and serve.
- Your wish list: What you want your child (and family) to become familiar with.

Having both in front of you shows where you are and where you're headed–and keeps growth gentle and realistic.

You don't need to tackle everything at once. Choose one or two foods from your wish list to explore each fortnight. These can be part of your child Food Familiarisation activities.

Once you've got your lists, think about creating a 2- or 4-week rotation. This might sound ambitious, but it's simply about re-using familiar foods in slightly different ways so your child can build recognition and confidence.

Repetition without boredom

Here's how it might look with something as simple as carrots:

- Week 1: Raw carrot sticks
- Week 2: Grated carrot in sandwiches or fritters
- Week 3: Roasted carrots with honey and herbs
- Week 4: Mashed carrots blended with sweet potato

Or chicken:

- Week 1: Whole roast chicken
- Week 2: Chicken schnitzel
- Week 3: Chicken nuggets
- Week 4: Chicken casserole

By repeating ingredients in different forms, you're helping your child learn how versatile food can be–without pressure or boredom.

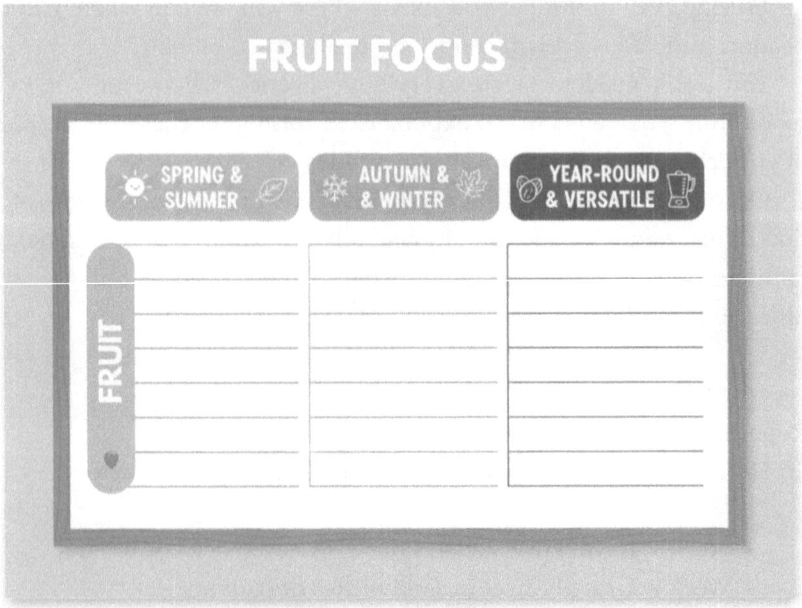

Fruit focus

Make a list of your favourite fruit options–some can be fresh, some frozen, some canned or bottled, and some dried. You may also include preparations that contain fruit, such as desserts, sorbets, smoothies and juices. Juices can be vitamin C-fortified, but because liquid fruit is easy to consume quickly, it's best limited to a small glass a day so it doesn't interfere with appetite.

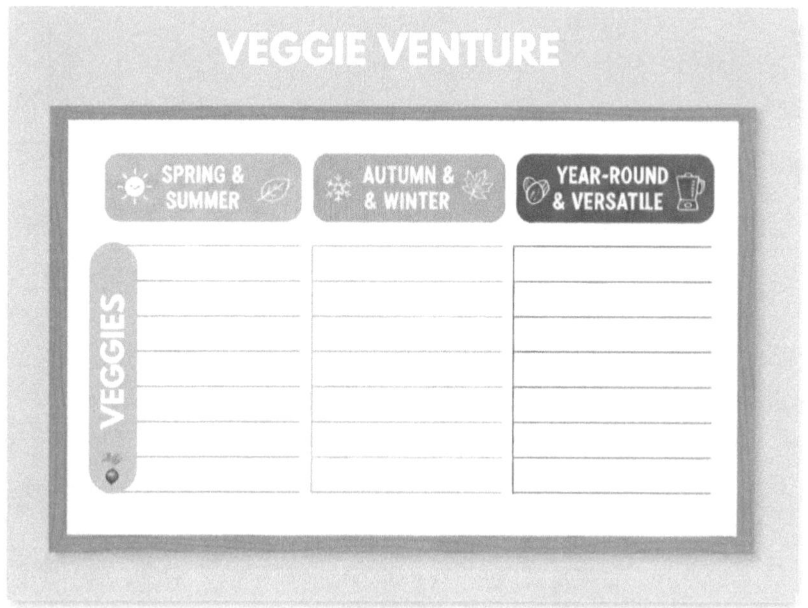

Veggie venture

Make a list of your go-to vegetables–those your child tolerates or enjoys–and those you'd love to introduce over time. Think beyond fresh produce: frozen, roasted, mashed, spiralised, blended, tinned or baked–every form counts. You can also include vegetable-based dishes like soups, fritters, patties and sauces.

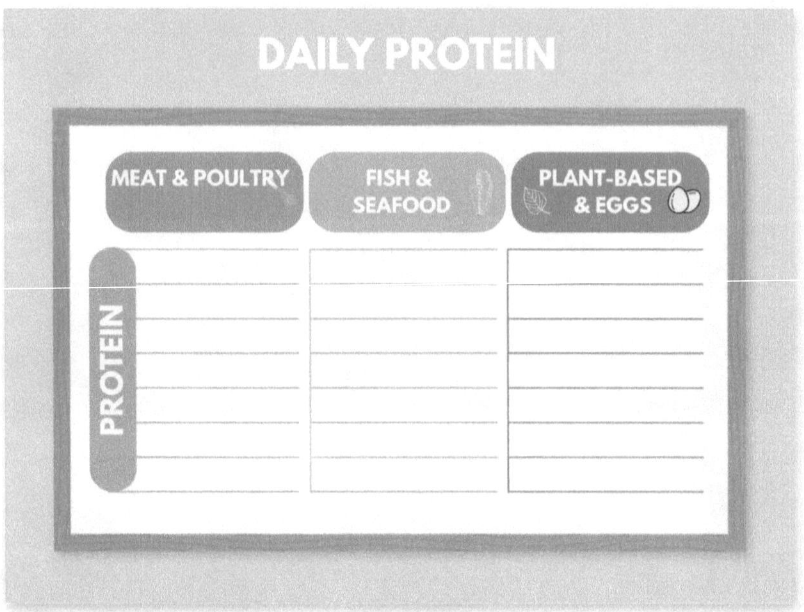

Daily protein

As you list your family's preferred proteins, include both the forms your child already accepts and the ones you'd like to introduce. Consider:

- **Meat, poultry, and fish**: grilling; steaming; poaching; braising; or pan-frying all create different textures and flavours.
- **Eggs:** versatile and quick–familiarise your child with boiled, scrambled, poached, or in omelettes and fritters.
- **Plant-based alternatives:** tofu, soybeans, or grains combined with legumes can create nutritious, flavourful vegetarian and vegan meals. Firm tofu fries beautifully with soy and honey, while softer versions work well in tempura or coconut-based dishes.

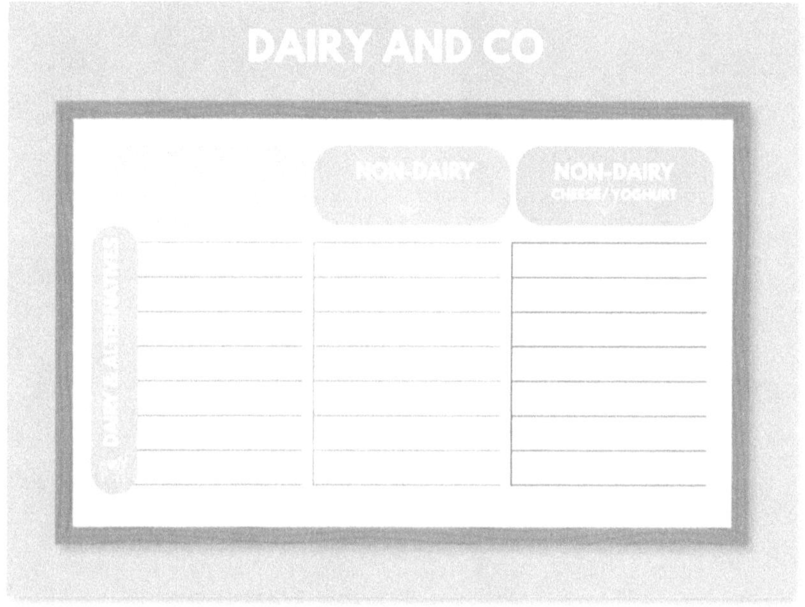

Dairy and Co

Navigating dairy and non-dairy options gives you the chance to offer your child a broad range of nutritious choices. Traditional dairy foods like milk, yoghurt, and cheese are rich in easily-absorbed calcium and quality protein–both essential for growing bodies. Fermented products such as yoghurt and kefir add the bonus of live bacteria that support gut health.

For families managing allergies, intolerances, or preferences, there are plenty of non-dairy alternatives worth exploring. Calcium-fortified options such as almond milk, soy yoghurt, or coconut-based products can provide excellent substitutes that still meet nutritional needs.

Finally, don't overlook custard, whether homemade or ready-made, with dairy or non-dairy milk. Smooth, sweet, and versatile, it can be a comforting way to add variety and enjoyment.

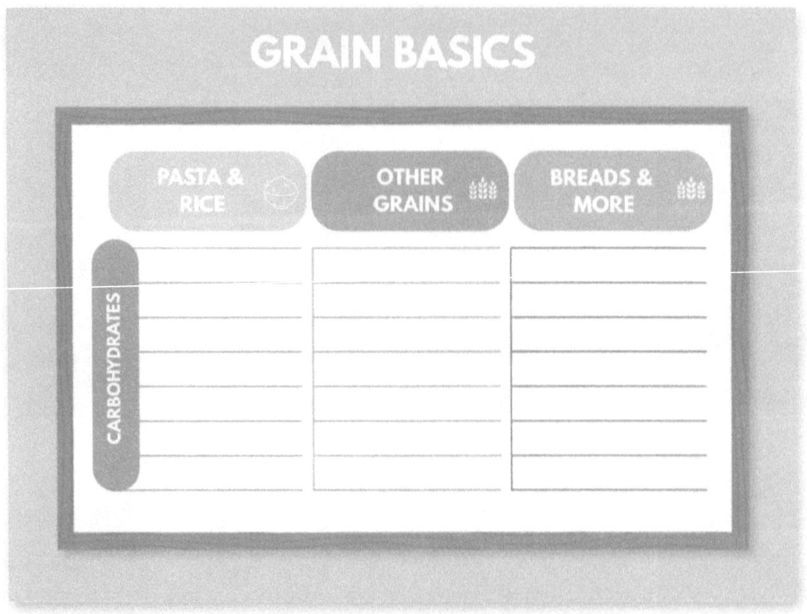

Grains basics

A well-planned list of grains–especially if you're looking for gluten-free options–makes it easier to decide what to introduce and how to use them. Most grains are simple to prepare, often just needing boiling water, which makes them an easy addition to your weekly meals.

Because most children are already familiar with bread, pasta, rice, or crackers, grains are a practical starting point when you're working on food variety. Wholemeal and wholegrain versions can be introduced early so children adjust to their taste and texture from the start.

Options to explore include:

- **Gluten-free grains:** rice (white, brown, wild, jasmine, basmati), quinoa, millet, and corn (including cornmeal and cornbread).
- **Traditional grains:** breads (white, whole wheat, multigrain, rye), pasta, oats, couscous, and bulgur.
- **Iron-**fortified bread.

These staples offer endless flexibility across meals, making it easier to expand your child's repertoire step by step.

ULTIMATE RELAXATION

Ultimate relaxation is where everything comes together. You and your child are no longer just surviving mealtimes–you're thriving in them. Meals are moments of connection, comfort, and even joy.

Your child trusts the Meal System completely: there will be food they can eat. You trust yourself completely in your role as the meal provider. You feel confident and steady, no longer second-guessing your decisions or battling doubt.

At this stage:

- Your child eats to appetite.
- You see flexibility in action–children can handle different settings, from school lunches to meals with extended family.
- Conversations flow freely at the table, and food has become part of the backdrop of family life, not the battleground.

This is the ultimate goal of the Reboots: not perfection, but calm and peace. A family table where everyone feels secure, respected, and connected.

Take a moment to notice how far you've come. This is the atmosphere that allows confidence, competence, and joy in eating to flourish–not just now, but for years to come.

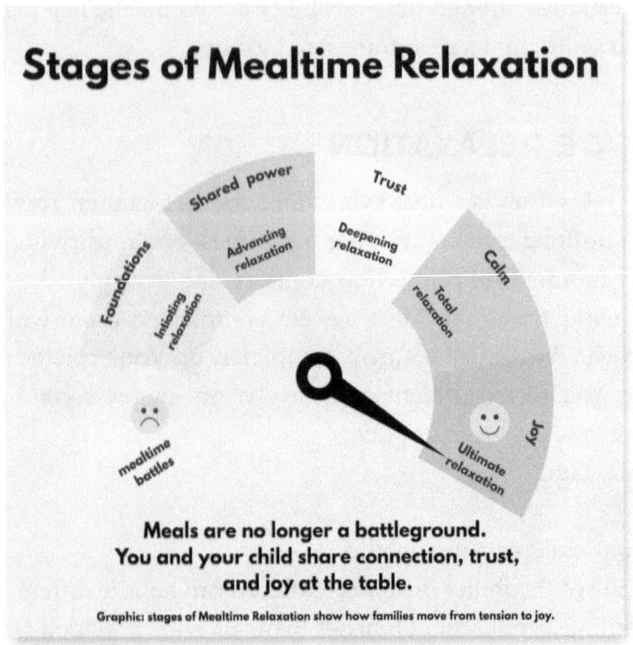

**Meals are no longer a battleground.
You and your child share connection, trust,
and joy at the table.**

Graphic: stages of Mealtime Relaxation show how families move from tension to joy.

REBOOT 5: LET'S GO!

Observe

- Are you organised for your food shopping, or does it feel a bit last-minute?
- Do you have a Meal System that helps you decide what to cook each week?
- Are there particular meals or dishes that feel meaningful in your home—ones you'd like to keep or bring back?
- Which ingredients are on heavy rotation? Are they serving you well, or do they need a refresh?
- Is there a food you'd love your child to become more familiar with—maybe for cultural reasons, nutrition, or just because you enjoy it?

Take action

1. Prepare your lists, including your shopping list.
2. Create a rotation over 2 weeks or 4 weeks, enabling your child to become more familiar with a wider range of food.

Assess progress

After working through Reboot 5, stand back and reflect on what has changed.

- Where have you and your child been successful?
- What still needs work?
- Is there anything you tried that didn't work–and what can you do instead?
- How do you feel?

Reboot
5

Progress Check-list 5

List of food/dishes that matter to your family	☐
Weekly Meal System	☐
Parents understand pairing and texture	☐
Parents rotate a growing list of food	☐
Children become familiar with a growing repertoire	☐

Turning ideas into everyday meals

SECTION 5: IN CONCLUSION

I've had the privilege of watching children who were once stubborn fussy eaters begin to enjoy meals, try new foods, and feel more at ease around the table. These changes happen in families where parents commit to creating a supportive environment. When it happens, it is extraordinary to witness your child turn a corner and become more open, more relaxed, and even curious about food.

For most families, this transformation does not happen overnight. Every bit of progress, no matter how small, matters. It is how children grow into adults who can feed themselves, enjoy food socially, and navigate eating without fear or stress.

By working through the seven continua, you have developed a clear understanding of where your child sits within extreme fussy eating. Through the five Reboots, you have gained a parenting plan to guide your child step by step towards a calmer, more confident relationship with food.

As a parent, you have:

- gained a deeper understanding of the complexities involved in fussy eating

- learned how to shape a supportive environment for your child's mealtime and food-related needs
- learned to pick your battles, using strong routines and clear expectations at mealtimes
- ended pressure around feeding
- reduced anxiety, including fight, flight, or freeze responses
- shared power with your child at mealtimes
- built trust around food
- empowered your child to solve food challenges across a wider range of environments
- begun teaching your child lifelong cooking and food skills, making food more approachable and manageable

These insights support a more nuanced and empathetic approach to mealtimes, helping create a better feeding dynamic between you and your child.

Pause for a moment of reflection.

Envisage your child as a teenager, effortlessly cooking up a simple pasta dish to share with your family or their peers. Picture your child as a young adult, laughing with friends over a restaurant dinner they navigated with ease. Then imagine your child as a fully grown adult, skilfully preparing their own meal.

All of this is a testament to the foundation you have established.

Allow yourself to revel in this accomplishment–your current efforts are moulding your child's future capabilities and building their confidence and competence in the realm of food and social interactions.

CHAPTER 18
HAPPIEST DINNERTIME EVER

'Our efforts haven't been in vain,' Olli's dad said with a laugh as he joined me on a call one evening.

He talked about how everything shifted once pressure was removed. Mealtimes stopped feeling charged. Olli no longer came to the table braced for battle, and his parents stopped monitoring every bite. Everyone felt more relaxed–calmer, lighter, and more connected.

But the real turning point, he said, was Food Familiarisation. At the beginning, there were so many foods Olli wouldn't even touch. Sundays became their familiarisation time–no expectations, no eating goals, just being together in the kitchen.

Slowly, things began to change. First, Olli accepted boiled eggs. Then bacon. Then peas. More recently, he and his dad mixed all three into rice at the bench, exploring how the foods could be combined and separated again. To everyone's surprise, it worked! Olli ate it happily and declared he had the best recipe! It was our happiest dinner ever!

'It's been life-changing,' his dad said. 'Meals don't

feel stressful anymore. They just feel… normal, our next step is going out to eat, this will be a new learning curve for Olli, I can't wait!'

YOUR DINNERTIME MOTTO

As you reach the final step of this parenting plan, consider creating a simple motto that captures the essence of what you've learned.

A dinnertime motto isn't just a pleasant phrase–it's a gentle reminder of the atmosphere you want to create. It brings focus back to what matters most: connection, calm, and shared enjoyment, rather than eating performance.

A motto can signal the tone of the meal, reduce pressure, and help everyone remember the values you're working toward. It can remind you to slow down, listen, and enjoy each other's company. It can guide children toward kindness, patience, and curiosity at the table.

Examples might include:

- 'We share and appreciate our meal together.'
- 'At dinner, we sit together, enjoy our meal, and talk about our day.'
- 'Our table is a calm place. We love each other's company at dinner.'

Choose something that reflects your family's personality and what you hope meals will feel like.

Writing your motto and placing it near the table creates a visual cue you can all rely on–especially during challenging moments. Over time, children internalise these values, carrying them into other settings and mealtimes.

A small motto can make a big difference. It anchors your family in shared purpose, supports calm behaviour, and helps protect the peaceful mealtime environment you've worked hard to build.

ANCHORS OF CONNECTION

Just as ships find stability with their anchors, you can create anchors that ground your mealtime experiences.

Anchoring, a technique derived from neuro-linguistic programming (NLP), offers a universal tool accessible to all. Imagine sharing a wonderful dinner with your children. Later, as you pass by them, gently rest your hand on their shoulder and express sentiments like, 'I had the best dinner with you tonight; I loved that moment with you' or 'What a fun conversation we had at dinner; it's precious having those moments with you'.

Anchoring emerges as a powerful means to reinforce positive emotions and experiences.

This practice establishes a profound connection between tactile sensation and uplifting feelings.

It transforms a simple touch into a trigger that can summon those heart-warming emotions at will. The beauty of this technique is that it links touch with deep feelings, making your relationships even more special.

STORIES OF THE MIND

Your child now can experience relaxed, practical, and non-pressured moments while managing food in their daily environment. You are now ready to bring stories of the mind to bedtime so the unconscious can also do its part. At this stage, I bring in hypnotherapy as an option for older children or guided meditation through bedtime stories.

While a child's imagination is limitless and metaphors are highly beneficial, I may keep the stories very literal for children with autism. Using a phase of body relaxation, through deep breathing and scanning the body for about 5 minutes, parents will bring their child to a state of comfortable, peaceful relaxation. It's now time to bring favourite characters to life as they invite your child on a wonderful drowsy-before-sleep adventure.

Parents can choose the lessons to be taught at that time of deep relaxation. Stories can be about sitting well and enjoying dinner with the family and told by the parent as if they were the character a long time ago. Stories don't have to be specifically about food; they can be about overcoming fears, increasing flexibility, sensing or tuning down body sensations and reducing the role of the fight, flight, or freeze responses children may have.

These new beliefs can then insert themselves naturally in all areas of the child's life, including food. Towards the end of the story, children can hear that they are going to enjoy a wonderful night's sleep. In the morning, they wake up, happy and energised, ready for new adventures.

EMBRACE THE PATH AHEAD

With each chapter of this book, you have stepped into unfamiliar territory and met challenges with courage and compassion. The insights you have gained will continue to evolve with you, because this journey is not static.

You now have a clear parenting plan to guide you through the twists and turns of feeding. Hold onto the moments you share around the table; they are where connection grows and family life quietly takes shape.

The transformation you are nurturing is not only about food. It is about creating safety, building trust, and strengthening the relationship you share with your learner-eater.

As each day ends and the next begins, remember that every meal offers another opportunity to practise calm, connection, and confidence. Over time, these small moments add up, helping your child grow into a confident and competent eater for life.

NOTES

2. THE PRESENTATION OF FUSSY EATING IN YOUR FAMILY

1. Zickgraf, H. F., Ellis, J. M., & Drummey, K. (2018). fussy eating in adulthood: A retrospective study of lifetime fussy eating in a community sample. Appetite, 126, 156-162

2. Carruth, B. R., Skinner, J., Houck, K., Moran, J. 3rd, & Coletta, F. (2012). Feeding behaviours and other motor development in healthy children (2-24 months). Appetite, 58(2), 704-708

3. Birch, L. L., McPhee, L., Shoba, B. C., Pirok, E., & Steinberg, L. (1987). What kind of exposure reduces children's food neophobia?: Looking vs. tasting. Appetite, 9(3), 171-178

4. Bárbara César Machado, Pedro Dias, Vânia Sousa Lima, Joana Campos, Sónia Gonçalves, Prevalence and correlates of picky eating in preschool-aged children: A population-based study,
   Eating Behaviors, Volume 22, 2016, Pages 16-21,ISSN 1471-0153,

5. Susan Dickerson Mayes, Hana Zickgraf, Atypical eating behaviors in children and adolescents with autism, ADHD, other disorders, and typical development, Research in Autism Spectrum Disorders, Volume 64, 2019, Pages 76-83, ISSN 1750-9467,

3. PRESSURES, EMOTIONS, AND CO-REGULATION WITH YOUR CHILD

1. Ritvo, E. R., Ritvo, R. A., Guthrie, D., & Ritvo, M. J. (2008). Leo Kanner, Hans Asperger, and the discovery of autism as a psychobiological disorder. Journal of the History of the behavioural Sciences, 44(3), 217-247

2. O'Brien, M., & Jordan, L. (2014). Mothers, blame and responsibility. Journal of gender studies, 23(3), 294-307

3. https://swnsdigital.com/us/2022/07/majority-of-parents-worry-their-kids-might-not-get-the-nutrients-they-need-because-of-their-fussiness-over-food/

4. Vereecken C, Rovner A, Maes L. Associations of parenting styles, parental feeding practices and child characteristics with young children's fruit and vegetable consumption. Appetite. 2010 Dec;55(3):589-96. doi: 10.1016/j.appet.2010.09.009. Epub 2010 Sep 16. PMID: 20849895.

5. Johnson SL, Birch LL. Parents' and children's adiposity and eating style. Pediatrics. 1994 Nov;94(5):653-61. PMID: 7936891.

6. Id.

4. PEACE OF MIND SOLUTIONS

1. Taylor CM, Emmett PM. Picky eating in children: causes and consequences. Proc

Nutr Soc. 2019 May;78(2):161-169. doi: 10.1017/S0029665118002586. Epub 2018 Nov 5. PMID: 30392488; PMCID: PMC6398579.

2. McKeen S., Young W., Mullaney J., Fraser K., McNabb W.C., Roy N.C. Infant Complementary Feeding of Prebiotics for the Microbiome and Immunity. Nutrients. 2019;11:364. doi: 10.3390/nu11020364.

3. Zhang YJ, Li S, Gan RY, Zhou T, Xu DP, Li HB. Impacts of gut bacteria on human health and diseases. Int J Mol Sci. 2015 Apr 2;16(4):7493-519. doi: 10.3390/ijms16047493. PMID: 25849657; PMCID: PMC4425030.

4. Anxiety might be alleviated by regulating gut bacteria. Review of studies suggests a potentially useful link between gut bacteria and mental disorders. BMJ-20/05/2019

5. S Salminen, A Ouwehand, Y Benno, Y.K Lee,Probiotics: how should they be defined?,Trends in Food Science & Technology,Volume 10, Issue 3,1999.

5. DIAGNOSTICS AND FEEDING THERAPY

1. Goday PS, Huh SY, Silverman A, Lukens CT, Dodrill P, Cohen SS, Delaney AL, Feuling MB, Noel RJ, Gisel E, Kenzer A, Kessler DB, Kraus de Camargo O, Browne J, Phalen JA. Pediatric Feeding Disorder: Consensus Definition and Conceptual Framework. J Pediatr Gastroenterol Nutr. 2019 Jan;68(1):124-129. doi: 10.1097/MPG.0000000000002188. PMID: 30358739; PMCID: PMC6314510.

2. Vasant DH, Hasan SS, Cruickshanks P, Whorwell PJ. Gut-focused hypnotherapy for children and adolescents with irritable bowel syndrome. Frontline Gastroenterol. 2020 Nov 23;12(7):570-577. doi: 10.1136/flgastro-2020-101679. PMID: 34917314; PMCID: PMC8640435.

6. CONTINUUM 1–PHYSICAL DISCOMFORT AND GENERAL HEALTH

1. Nelson SP, Chen EH, Syniar GM, Christoffel KK. Prevalence of symptoms of gastroesophageal reflux during infancy. A paediatric practice-based survey. Arch Pediatr Adolesc Med. 1997;151(6):569-572. doi:10.1001/archpedi.1997.02170430031005

2. Rosen R, Vandenplas Y, Singendonk M, et al. paediatric Gastroesophageal Reflux Clinical Practice Guidelines: Joint Recommendations of the North American Society for paediatric Gastroenterology, Hepatology, and Nutrition and the European Society for paediatric Gastroenterology, Hepatology, and Nutrition. J Pediatr Gastroenterol Nutr. 2018;66(3):516-554. doi:10.1097/MPG.0000000000001889

3. Sullivan, P. B. (2008). Gastrointestinal disorders in children with neurodevelopmental disabilities. Dev Disabil Res Rev, 14(2), 128-136. doi: 10.1002/ddrr.18

4. Vandenplas, Y., Abkari, A., Bellaiche, M., Benninga, M., Chouraqui, J. P., Çokura, F.,... & Hegar, B. (2015). Prevalence and health outcomes of functional gastrointestinal symptoms in infants from birth to 12 months of age. Journal of paediatric gastroenterology and nutrition, 61(5), 531-537

5. Savage, J. H., & Johns, C. B. (2015). Food allergy: epidemiology and natural history. Immunology and allergy clinics of North America, 35(1), 45-59

6. Garcia, J. (1989). Food for Tolman: Cognition and cathexis in concert. In T. Archer & L.-G. Nilsson (Eds.), Aversion, avoidance, and anxiety: Perspectives on aversively motivated behaviour (pp. 45–85). Lawrence Erlbaum Associates, Inc.

7. Zucker N, Mauro C, Craske M, Wagner HR, Datta N, Hopkins H, Caldwell K, Kiridly A, Marsan S, Maslow G, Mayer E, Egger H. Acceptance-based interoceptive exposure for young children with functional abdominal pain. Behav Res Ther. 2017 Oct;97:200-212. doi: 10.1016/j.brat.2017.07.009. Epub 2017 Jul 29. PMID: 28826066; PMCID: PMC5786377.

8. Theresa L, Mary T, Kendra H, Heather J, Rachel L, et al. (2017) Picky Eating and the Associated Nutritional Consequences. J Food Nutr Disord 6:3. doi: 10.4172/2324-9323.1000227

   Theresa L, Mary T, Kendra H, Heather J, Rachel L, et al. (2017) Picky Eating and the Associated Nutritional Consequences. J Food Nutr Disord 6:3. doi: 10.4172/2324-9323.1000227

9. Grippaudo C, Paolantonio EG, Antonini G, Saulle R, La Torre G, Deli R. Association between oral habits, mouth breathing and malocclusion. Acta Otorhinolaryngol Ital. 2016 Oct;36(5):386-394. doi: 10.14639/0392-100X-770. PMID: 27958599; PMCID: PMC5225794.

10. Abreu RR1, Rocha RL, Lamounier JA, Guerra AF.. Etiology, clinical manifestations and concurrent findings in mouth-breathing children. J Pediatr (Rio J).2008;(Nov-Dec;84(6):529-35.

11. Shah SS, Nankar MY, Bendgude VD, Shetty BR. Orofacial Myofunctional Therapy in Tongue Thrust Habit: A Narrative Review. Int J Clin Pediatr Dent. 2021 Mar-Apr;14(2):298-303. doi: 10.5005/jp-journals-10005-1926. PMID: 34413610; PMCID: PMC8343673.

12. Mousa H, Hassan M. Gastroesophageal Reflux Disease. Pediatr Clin North Am. 2017 Jun;64(3):487-505. doi: 10.1016/j.pcl.2017.01.003. PMID: 28502434; PMCID: PMC6509354.

13. Id.

14. Sano M, Sano S, Oka N, Yoshino K, Kato T. Increased oxygen load in the prefrontal cortex from mouth breathing: a vector-based near-infrared spectroscopy study. Neuroreport. 2013 Dec 4;24(17):935-40. doi: 10.1097/WNR.0000000000000008. PMID: 24169579; PMCID: PMC4047298.

15. Liu Y, Zhou JR, Xie SQ, Yang X, Chen JL. The Effects of Orofacial Myofunctional Therapy on Children with OSAHS's Craniomaxillofacial Growth: A Systematic Review. Children (Basel). 2023 Mar 31;10(4):670. doi: 10.3390/children10040670. PMID: 37189919; PMCID: PMC10136844.

16. Thomas JJ, Brigham KS, Sally ST, Hazen EP, Eddy KT. Case 18-2017 - An 11-Year-Old Girl with Difficulty Eating after a Choking Incident. N Engl J Med. 2017 Jun 15;376(24):2377-2386. doi: 10.1056/NEJMcpc1616394. PMID: 28614676; PMCID: PMC5724771.

17. Nicely, T.A., Lane-Loney, S., Masciulli, E. et al. Prevalence and characteristics of avoidant/restrictive food intake disorder in a cohort of young patients in day treatment for eating disorders. J Eat Disord 2, 21 (2014). https://doi.org/10.1186/s40337-014-0021-3

18. Rachidi*, L.., Jbilou, W. ., Youssra, A. ., Aftahi, F. ., Serhani, H. ., & Benjelloun, G. . (2022). Phagophobia in A 6-Year-Old Child : Case Report. Clinical Medicine And Health Research Journal, 2(5), 195–197. https://doi.org/10.18535/cmhrj.v2i5.85

19. Satter, E. (1986). The feeding relationship: Problems and interventions. Journal of paediatrics, 109(2), 194-198. doi: 10.1016/S0022-3476(86)80262-5

20. Id.

21. https://www.ncbi.nlm.nih.gov/books/NBK536881/

7. CONTINUUM 2–APPETITE

1. Birch LL, McPhee L, Sullivan S. Children's food intake following drinks sweetened with sucrose or aspartame: time course effects. Physiol Behav. 1989 Feb;45(2):387-95. doi: 10.1016/0031-9384(89)90145-5. PMID: 2756027.

2. Birch LL, Johnson SL, Andresen G, Peters JC, Schulte MC. The variability of young children's energy intake. N Engl J Med. 1991;324(4):232–5.

3. Birch LL, Fisher JO. Development of Eating behaviours among Children and Adolescents. Pediatrics. 1998;101(3 part 2):539–549.

4. Polivy, J., Coleman, J., & Herman, C. P. (2005). The effect of deprivation on food cravings and eating behaviour in restrained and unrestrained eaters. Appetite, 44(2), 133-141. doi: 10.1016/j.appet.2004.09.006

5. Taylor, C.M., Steer, C.D., Hays, N.P. *et al.* Growth and body composition in children who are picky eaters: a longitudinal view. *Eur J Clin Nutr* **73**, 869–878 (2019). https://doi.org/10.1038/s41430-018-0250-7

6. Leung AK, Marchand V, Sauve RS; Canadian Paediatric Society, Nutrition and Gastroenterology Committee. The 'picky eater': The toddler or preschooler who does not eat. Paediatr Child Health. 2012 Oct;17(8):455-60. doi: 10.1093/pch/17.8.455. PMID: 24082809; PMCID: PMC3474391.

7. Kerzner B, Milano K, MacLean WC Jr, Berall G, Stuart S, Chatoor I. A practical approach to classifying and managing feeding difficulties. Pediatrics. 2015 Feb;135(2):344-53. doi: 10.1542/peds.2014-1630. Epub 2015 Jan 5. PMID: 25560449.

8. https://www.mayoclinic.org/healthy-lifestyle/infant-and-toddler-health/expert-answers/infant-growth/faq-20058037

9. Leung AK, Marchand V, Sauve RS; Canadian Paediatric Society, Nutrition and Gastroenterology Committee. The 'picky eater': The toddler or preschooler who does not eat. Paediatr Child Health. 2012 Oct;17(8):455-60. doi: 10.1093/pch/17.8.455. PMID: 24082809; PMCID: PMC3474391.

10. Https://www.rch.org.au/uploadedFiles/Main/Content/childgrowth/Healthprofessionals_QAChild_growth_monitoring_Nov2013.pdf

11. Mascola AJ, Bryson SW, Agras WS. Picky eating during childhood: a longitudinal study to age 11 years. Eat Behav. 2010 Dec;11(4):253-7. doi: 10.1016/j.eatbeh.2010.05.006. Epub 2010 May 27. PMID: 20850060; PMCID: PMC2943861..

12. Farrow CV, Coulthard H. Relationships between sensory sensitivity, anxiety and selective eating in children. Appetite. 2012 Jun;58(3):842-6. doi: 10.1016/j.appet.2012.01.017. Epub 2012 Feb 2. PMID: 22326881.

13. Galloway AT, Fiorito LM, Francis LA, Birch LL. 'Finish your soup': counterproductive effects of pressuring children to eat on intake and affect. Appetite. 2006 May;46(3):318-23. doi: 10.1016/j.appet.2006.01.019. Epub 2006 Apr 19. PMID: 16626838; PMCID: PMC2604806.

14. Isguven P, Arslanoglu I, Erol M, Yildiz M, Adal E, Erguven M. Serum levels of ghrelin, leptin, IGF-I, IGFBP-3, insulin, thyroid hormones and cortisol in prepubertal children with iron deficiency. Endocr J. 2007 Dec;54(6):985-90. doi: 10.1507/endocrj.k07-031. Epub 2007 Nov 12. PMID: 17998761.

15. Kelesidis T, Kelesidis I, Chou S, Mantzoros CS. Narrative review: the role of leptin in human physiology: emerging clinical applications. Ann Intern Med. 2010 Jan 19;152(2):93-100. doi: 10.7326/0003-4819-152-2-201001190-00008. PMID: 20083828; PMCID: PMC2829242.

16. Kojima M., Hosoda H., Date Y., Nakazato M., Matsuo H., Kangawa K. Ghrelin is a

growth-hormone-releasing acylated peptide from stomach. Nature. 1999;402:656–660. [PubMed] [Google Scholar]

17. Khan Y, Tisman G. Pica in iron deficiency: a case series. J Med Case Rep. 2010 Mar 12;4:86. doi: 10.1186/1752-1947-4-86. PMID: 20226051; PMCID: PMC2850349.

18. Bener A, Kamal M, Bener H, Bhugra D. Higher prevalence of iron deficiency as strong predictor of attention deficit hyperactivity disorder in children. Ann Med Health Sci Res. 2014 Sep;4(Suppl 3):S291-7. doi: 10.4103/2141-9248.141974. PMID: 25364604; PMCID: PMC4212392.

19. Abu-Ouf NM, Jan MM. The impact of maternal iron deficiency and iron deficiency anemia on child's health. Saudi Med J. 2015 Feb;36(2):146-9. doi: 10.15537/smj.2015.2.10289. PMID: 25719576; PMCID: PMC4375689.

20. Royal Children's Hospital Melbourne. *Iron deficiency*. Clinical Practice Guidelines.

21. Taylor CM, Northstone K, Wernimont SM, Emmett PM. Macro- and micronutrient intakes in picky eaters: a cause for concern? Am J Clin Nutr. 2016 Dec;104(6):1647-1656. doi: 10.3945/ajcn.116.137356. Epub 2016 Nov 9. PMID: 27935522; PMCID: PMC5118732.

22. Chao HC, Lu JJ, Yang CY, Yeh PJ, Chu SM. Serum Trace Element Levels and Their Correlation with Picky Eating Behavior, Development, and Physical Activity in Early Childhood. Nutrients. 2021 Jul 2;13(7):2295. doi: 10.3390/nu13072295. PMID: 34371805; PMCID: PMC8308333.

23. Risso, D.; Drayna, D.; Morini, G. Alteration, Reduction and Taste Loss: Main Causes and Potential Implications on Dietary Habits. Nutrients 2020, 12, 3284. https://doi.org/10.3390/nu12113284

24. Vreugdenhil M, Akkermans MD, van der Merwe LF, van Elburg RM, van Goudoever JB, Brus F. Prevalence of Zinc Deficiency in Healthy 1–3-Year-Old Children from Three Western European Countries. Nutrients. 2021; 13(11):3713. https://doi.org/10.3390/nu13113713

25. Drugs and Appetite: An Overview of Appetite Stimulants in the Pediatric Patient Kathleen Gura, PharmD, and Roselle Ciccone, PharmD candidate

26. Wu KL, Rayner CK, Chuah SK, et al. Effects of ginger on gastric emptying and motility in healthy humans. Eur J Gastroenterol Hepatol. 2008;20:436-440

27. Hveem K, Jones KL, Chatterton BE, Horowitz M. Scintigraphic measurement of gastric emptying and ultrasonographic assessment of antral area: relation to appetite. Gut. 1996;38:816-821

8. CONTINUUM 3–EATING SKILLS

1. Białek-Dratwa A, Szczepańska E, Szymańska D, Grajek M, Krupa-Kotara K, Kowalski O. Neophobia-A Natural Developmental Stage or Feeding Difficulties for Children? Nutrients. 2022 Apr 6;14(7):1521. doi: 10.3390/nu14071521. PMID: 35406134; PMCID: PMC9002550.

2. https://www.who.int/health-topics/complementary-feeding#tab=tab_2

3. Northstone K, Emmett P, Nethersole F; ALSPAC Study Team. Avon Longitudinal Study of Pregnancy and Childhood. The effect of age of introduction to lumpy solids on foods eaten and reported feeding difficulties at 6 and 15 months. J Hum Nutr Diet. 2001 Feb;14(1):43-54. doi: 10.1046/j.1365-277x.2001.00264.x. PMID: 11301932.

4. Kerwin, Marylouise. (2003). Pediatric Feeding Problems: A behaviour Analytic Approach to Assessment and Treatment. The behaviour Analyst Today. 4. 10.1037/h0100114.

5. Beauchamp, G. K., Mennella, J. A., & Johnson, A. (2010). Early flavour learning and its impact on later feeding behaviour. Journal of paediatric gastroenterology and nutrition, 51(Supplement 1), S180-S182.

6. Savage JS, Fisher JO, Birch LL. Parental influence on eating behavior: conception to adolescence. J Law Med Ethics. 2007 Spring;35(1):22-34. doi: 10.1111/j.1748-720X.2007.00111.x. PMID: 17341215; PMCID: PMC2531152.

7. Drewnowski, A., & Goméz-Carneros, C. (2000). Bitter taste, phytonutrients, and the consumer: a review. The American journal of clinical nutrition, 72(6), 1424-1435.

8. Hepper PG, Wells DL, Dornan JC, Lynch C. Long-term flavor recognition in humans with prenatal garlic experience. Dev Psychobiol. 2013 Jul;55(5):568-74. doi: 10.1002/dev.21059. Epub 2012 Jul 2. PMID: 22753112.

9. Calancie L, Keyserling TC, Taillie LS, Robasky K, Patterson C, Ammerman AS, Schisler JC. *TAS2R38* Predisposition to Bitter Taste Associated with Differential Changes in Vegetable Intake in Response to a Community-Based Dietary Intervention. G3 (Bethesda). 2018 May 31;8(6):2107-2119. doi: 10.1534/g3.118.300547. PMID: 29686110; PMCID: PMC5982837.

10. ladik, Marcel. (2002). Le comportement alimentaire des primates : de la socio-écologie régime éclectique des hominidés

11. In-Mouth Volatile Production from Brassica Vegetables (Cauliflower) and Associations with Liking in an Adult/Child Cohort. Damian Frank, Udayasika Piyasiri, Nicholas Archer, Jessica Heffernan, and Astrid A. M. Poelman.Journal of Agricultural and Food Chemistry 2021 69 (39), 11646-11655. DOI: 10.1021/acs.jafc.1c03889

9. CONTINUUM 4–SENSORY SENSITIVITIES AND OVERLOAD

1. Shimizu VT, Bueno OF, Miranda MC. Sensory processing abilities of children with ADHD. Braz J Phys Ther. 2014 Jul-Aug;18(4):343-52. doi: 10.1590/bjpt-rbf.2014.0043. Epub 2014 Jul 25. PMID: 25076000; PMCID: PMC4183255.

2. Steinsbekk, S., Bonneville-Roussy, A., Fildes, A. et al. Child and parent predictors of picky eating from preschool to school age. Int J Behav Nutr Phys Act 14, 87 (2017). https://doi.org/10.1186/s12966-017-0542-7

3. Cervin M. Sensory Processing Difficulties in Children and Adolescents with Obsessive-Compulsive and Anxiety Disorders. Res Child Adolesc Psychopathol. 2023 Feb;51(2):223-232. doi: 10.1007/s10802-022-00962-w. Epub 2022 Sep 23. PMID: 36149521; PMCID: PMC9867656.

4. Fine LG, Riera CE. Sense of Smell as the Central Driver of Pavlovian Appetitebehaviourin Mammals. Front Physiol. 2019 Sep 18;10:1151. doi: 10.3389/fphys.2019.01151. PMID: 31620009; PMCID: PMC6759725.

5. Shwin C, Chapman E, Howells J, Rhydderch D, Walker I, Baron-Cohen S. Enhanced olfactory sensitivity in autism spectrum conditions. Mol Autism. 2014 Nov 20;5:53. doi: 10.1186/2040-2392-5-53. PMID: 25908951; PMCID: PMC4407326.

6. Coulthard H, Harris G, Fogel A. Association between tactile over-responsivity and vegetable consumption early in the introduction of solid foods and its variation with age. Matern Child Nutr. 2016 Oct;12(4):848-59. doi: 10.1111/mcn.12228. Epub 2016 Jan 21. PMID: 26792423; PMCID: PMC6860046.

7. Ross CF, Surette VA, Bernhard CB, Smith-Simpson S, Lee J, Russell CG, Keast R. Development and application of specific questions to classify a child as food texture sensitive. J Texture Stud. 2022 Feb;53(1):3-17. doi: 10.1111/jtxs.12627. Epub 2021 Sep 5. PMID: 34435671.

10. CONTINUUM 5–FOOD NEOPHOBIA AND DISGUST

1. Faith MS, Heo M, Keller KL, Pietrobelli A. Child food neophobia is heritable, associated with less compliant eating, and moderates familial resemblance for BMI. Obesity. 2013;21(8):1650–1655. http://doi.org/10.1002/oby.20369. [PMC free article] [PubMed] [Google Scholar]
2. Birch LL, Fisher JO. Development of eating behaviors among children and adolescents. Pediatrics. 1998;101(3 Pt 2):539–549. [PubMed] [Google Scholar]
3. Natalie Rigal, la naissance du goût. Editions Noesis, 2000
4. Białek-Dratwa A, Szczepańska E, Szymańska D, Grajek M, Krupa-Kotara K, Kowalski O. Neophobia-A Natural Developmental Stage or Feeding Difficulties for Children? Nutrients. 2022 Apr 6;14(7):1521. doi: 10.3390/nu14071521. PMID: 35406134; PMCID: PMC9002550.
5. Natalie Rigal, la naissance du goût. Editions Noesis, 2000
6. Moding KJ, Stifter CA. Stability of food neophobia from infancy through early childhood. Appetite. 2016 Feb 1;97:72-8. doi: 10.1016/j.appet.2015.11.016. Epub 2015 Dec 2. PMID: 26612089; PMCID: PMC4706782.
7. Marcontell DK, Laster AE, Johnson J. Cognitive-behavioral treatment of food neophobia in adults. J Anxiety Disord. 2003;17(2):243-51. doi: 10.1016/s0887-6185(01)00090-1. PMID: 12614666.
8. Natalie Rigal, la naissance du goût. Editions Noesis, 2000
9. Wang, Yx., Luo, W., Sun, Xx. *et al.* The prevalence and factors associated with food neophobia in preschool children: a cross-sectional study in Jiangsu Province, China. *BMC Public Health* **25**, 661 (2025). https://doi.org/10.1186/s12889-025-21924-z
10. Susan L Johnson, Patricia L Davies, Richard E Boles, William J Gavin, Laura L Bellows,
    Young Children's Food Neophobia Characteristics and Sensory Behaviors Are Related to Their Food Intake1,2, The Journal of Nutrition,Volume 145, Issue 11, 2015
11. Food neophobia: Higher responsiveness to sensory properties but low engagement with foods generally. John Prescott, Sok L. Chheang, Sara R. Jaeger. First published: 23 June 2022 https://doi.org/10.1111/joss.1277
12. Moding KJ, Birch LL, Stifter CA. Infant temperament and feeding history predict infants' responses to novel foods. Appetite. 2014;83:218–225. http://doi.org/10.1016/j.appet.2014.08.030. [PMC free article] [PubMed] [Google Scholar]
13. Pliner P, Loewen ER. Temperament and food neophobia in children and their mothers. Appetite. 1997;28(3):239–254. http://doi.org/10.1006/appe.1996.0078. [PubMed] [Google Scholar]
14. Rozin, P., Haidt, J., & McCauley, C. R. (2008). Disgust.
    In Handbook of Emotions (3rd ed.), edited by Lewis, Haviland-Jones & Barrett.

11. CONTINUUM 6– TEMPERAMENT AND EATING

1. Saudino KJ. behavioural genetics and child temperament. J Dev Behav Pediatr. 2005 Jun;26(3):214-23. doi: 10.1097/00004703-200506000-00010. PMID: 15956873; PMCID: PMC1188235.

2. Linscheid TR, Lumeng JC, Appugliese D, Kaciroti N. Temperament and fussy eating in early childhood. J Dev Behav Pediatr. 2018 Jun;39(5):365-372. doi: 10.1097/DBP.0000000000000547. PMID: 29432416

3. Herle, M., Fildes, A., van Jaarsveld, C. H., & Llewellyn, C. H. (2019). Emotional and behavioural predictors of fussy eating in childhood. Journal of paediatric Psychology, 44(8), 950-960. doi: 10.1093/jpepsy/jsz039

4. Bleck J., DeBate R.D. Exploring the co-morbidity of attention-deficit/hyperactivity disorder with eating disorders and disordered eating behaviors in a nationally representative community-based sample. *Eat. Behav.* 2013;14(3):390–393.

13. REBOOT 1–BUILDING THE FOUNDATIONS FOR CALM EATING

1. Savastio S, Bellone S, Baldelli R, Ferraris M, Lapidari A, Zanetta F, Sogni S, Petri A, Bona G. Role of ghrelin in the regulation of appetite in children. Minerva Pediatr. 2006 Feb;58(1):21-6. PMID: 16541004.

2. Julie M. Frecka and Richard D. Mattes. Possible entrainment of ghrelin to habitual meal patterns in humans. Am J Physiol Gastrointest Liver Physiol294: G699–G707, 2008.First published January 10, 2008; doi:10.1152/ajpgi.00448.2007.0193-1857/08

3. Rangan AM, Randall D, Hector DJ, Gill TP, Webb KL. Consumption of 'extra' foods by Australian children: types, quantities and contribution to energy and nutrient intakes. Eur J Clin Nutr. 2008 Mar;62(3):356-64. doi: 10.1038/sj.ejcn.1602720. Epub 2007 Mar 14. PMID: 17356553.

4. Chao HC. Association of Picky Eating with Growth, Nutritional Status, Development, Physical Activity, and Health in Preschool Children. Front Pediatr. 2018 Feb 12;6:22. doi: 10.3389/fped.2018.00022. PMID: 29484290; PMCID: PMC5816267.

14. REBOOT 2–SHARING POWER WITHOUT LOSING YOUR ROLE

1. Fries LR, van der Horst K. Parental feeding practices and associations with Children's food acceptance and picky eating. Nestle Nutr Inst Workshop Ser. 2019;91:31–9.

2. Di Domenico SI, Ryan RM. The Emerging Neuroscience of Intrinsic Motivation: A New Frontier in Self-Determination Research. Front Hum Neurosci. 2017 Mar 24;11:145. doi: 10.3389/fnhum.2017.00145. PMID: 28392765; PMCID: PMC5364176.

3. Di Domenico SI, Ryan RM. The Emerging Neuroscience of Intrinsic Motivation: A New Frontier in Self-Determination Research. Front Hum Neurosci. 2017 Mar 24;11:145. doi: 10.3389/fnhum.2017.00145. PMID: 28392765; PMCID: PMC5364176.

4. Michal Maimaran, Ayelet Fishbach, If It's Useful and You Know It, Do You Eat? Preschoolers Refrain from Instrumental Food, Journal of Consumer Research, Volume 41, Issue 3, 1 October 2014, Pages 642–655, https://doi.org/10.1086/677224

5. Id.

6. Birch, L. L., & Marlin, D. W. (1982). I don't like it; I never tried it: Effects of exposure on two-year-old children's food preferences. Appetite, 3(4), 353-360.

7. Smith, R., Brown, K., & Jones, M. (2022). The role of food rewards in shaping children's food preferences: A longitudinal study. Appetite, 5(1), 18-26.

8. Birch LL, Zimmerman SI, Hind H. The Influence of Social-affective Context on

Preschool Children's Food Preferences. Child Development. 1980;51:856–861. [Google Scholar]

9. Jansen PW, Derks IPM, Mou Y, van Rijen EHM, Gaillard R, Micali N, Voortman T, Hillegers MHJ. Associations of parents' use of food as reward with children's eating behaviour and BMI in a population-based cohort. Pediatr Obes. 2020 Nov;15(11):e12662. doi: 10.1111/ijpo.12662. Epub 2020 Jun 16. PMID: 32548949; PMCID: PMC7583369.

10. Ann Marie Barry (2009) Mirror Neurons: How We Become What We See, Visual Communication Quarterly, 16:2, 79-89, DOI: 10.1080/15551390902803820

11. Palfreyman Z, Haycraft E, Meyer C. Parental modelling of eating behaviours: observational validation of the Parental Modelling of Eating Behaviours scale (PARM). Appetite. 2015 Mar;86:31-7. doi: 10.1016/j.appet.2014.08.008. Epub 2014 Aug 8. PMID: 25111293.

12. Sweetman C, McGowan L, Croker H, Cooke L. Characteristics of family mealtimes affecting children's vegetable consumption and liking. J Am Diet Assoc. 2011 Feb;111(2):269-73. doi: 10.1016/j.jada.2010.10.050. PMID: 21272701.

13. SCALE Duke, M.P., Lazarus, A., & Fivush, R. (2008). Knowledge of family history as a clinically useful index of psychological well-being and prognosis: A brief report. Psychotherapy Theory, Research, Practice, Training, 45, 268-272.

14. Snow, C.E. and Beals, D.E. (2006), Mealtime talk that supports literacy development. New Directions for Child and Adolescent Development, 2006: 51-66.

15. REBOOT 3–FROM REFUSAL TO FAMILIARITY

1. Coulthard H, Thakker D. Enjoyment of tactile play is associated with lower food neophobia in preschool children. J Acad Nutr Diet. 2015 Jul;115(7):1134-40. doi: 10.1016/j.jand.2015.02.020. Epub 2015 Apr 29. PMID: 25935569.

2. Marsha Dunn Klein, https://getpermissioninstitute.com/

3. Utter J, Larson N, Laska MN, Winkler M, Neumark-Sztainer D. Self-Perceived Cooking Skills in Emerging Adulthood Predict Better Dietary behaviours and Intake 10 Years Later: A Longitudinal Study. J Nutr Educ Behav. 2018 May;50(5):494-500. doi: 10.1016/j.jneb.2018.01.021. Epub 2018 Mar 7. PMID: 29525525; PMCID: PMC6086120.

4. Gibbons A. Paleoanthropology. Food for thought Science. 2007;316:1558–1560. [PubMed] [Google Scholar]

5. Ross, Carolyn & Bernhard, Ben & Smith-Simpson, Sarah. (2019). Parent-reported ease of eating foods of different textures in young children with Down syndrome. Journal of Texture Studies. 50. 10.1111/jtxs.12410.

16. REBOOT 4–WHAT YOU SAY MATTERS MORE THAN YOU THINK

1. **Phelan, T. W.** (2016). *1–2–3 Magic: 3-Step Discipline for Calm, Effective, and Happy Parenting.* Naperville, IL: Sourcebooks.

2. **Hawton, M.** (2013). *Talk Less, Listen More: Solutions for Children's Difficult Behaviour.* Byron Bay, NSW: Exisle Publishing.

3. https://www.gordontraining.com/thomas-gordon/about-dr-thomas-gordon-1918-2002/

4. Language of listening. https://www.languageoflistening.com/
5. https://autismawarenesscentre.com/speakers/jed-baker/

17. REBOOT 5–TURNING IDEAS
INTO EVERYDAY MEALS

1. Savage JS, Fisher JO, Birch LL. Parental influence on eating behavior: conception to adolescence. J Law Med Ethics. 2007 Spring;35(1):22-34. doi: 10.1111/j.1748-720X.2007.00111.x. PMID: 17341215; PMCID: PMC2531152.

APPENDIX

FOOD GUIDE, IRON SOURCES, HEALTHY FATS, COOKING METHODS

	Spring, Summer	Autumn, Winter	Other Fruit Options
FRUIT	**Fresh** Apricot Banana Blackberry Blueberry Cantaloupe Cherry Feijoa Fig Guava Grape Kiwi Lychee Mango Melon Nectarine Papaya Passion Fruit Peach Persimmon Pineapple Plum Quince Raspberry Strawberry Watermelon	**Fresh** Apple Avocado Custard Apple Date Grapefruit Kiwi Kumquat Lemon Mandarin Orange Passion Fruit (late winter) Pear Persimmon Pomegranate Quince Tamarillo Tangerine	**Dried** Apple (rings or chips) Apricot Banana (chips or slices) Coconut (flakes or shredded) Cranberry Date Fig Goji Berry Mango (strips or slices) Pineapple (rings or chunks) Prunes Raisin Sultana **Frozen** Acai (packets) Banana (slices or chunks) Blueberry Cherry Coconut (chunks or shredded) Cranberry Mango (chunks or slices) Peach (slices or halves) Pineapple (chunks or slices) Raspberry Strawberry Mixed Berries **Puréed** Apple (applesauce) Apricot Banana Blackberry Blueberry Coconut (cream or purée) Date (paste) Guava (paste) Mango Passion Fruit (pulp) Peach Pear Pineapple Plum Prunes Raspberry Strawberry

Dark Leafy, Cruciferous

Broccoli
Brussels sprouts
Cabbage
Cauliflower
Kale
Silverbeet
Spinach

Roots, Tubers & Bulbs

Beetroot
Carrot
Garlic
Onion
Potato
Shallot
Swede
Sweet potato
Turnip

Others

Leek
Snow peas
Fennel

Fruiting Vegetables

Avocado
Capsicum (bell pepper)
Corn
Cucumber
Eggplant (aubergine)
Squash
Sweet corn
Tomato
Zucchini

Legumes & Pods

Green beans
Peas
Sugar snap peas

Leafy & Tender Greens

Lettuce
Rocket (arugula)
Watercress
Bok choy

Other

Celery
Spring onion

Dried

Carrot (chips or slices)
Tomato (sun-dried or flakes)
Spinach (flakes)
Kale (chips)
Beetroot (chips or powder)
Onion (flakes or powder)
Garlic (granules or powder)
Mushroom (slices or powder)
Peas (split or whole, dried)
Corn (freeze-dried kernels)
Seaweed (nori, kelp, or wakame)

Frozen

Broccoli (florets)
Cauliflower (florets)
Carrot (slices or diced)
Spinach (chopped)
Kale (chopped)
Peas (shelled)
Corn (kernels)
Green beans
Brussels sprouts
Sweet corn
Zucchini (slices or spirals)
Bell pepper (slices or diced)
Snow peas (whole)
Sugar snap peas (whole)
Edamame (shelled)
Artichoke hearts (halved)
Asparagus (spears)

Puréed /tinned

Tomato (purée or paste)
Pumpkin (purée)
Sweet potato (purée)
Carrot (purée)
Spinach (purée)
Pea (purée)
Cauliflower (purée or rice)
Broccoli (purée)
Beetroot (purée)
Avocado (mash or purée)
Zucchini (purée)
Eggplant (baba ganoush)
Butternut squash (purée)
Corn (creamed corn)

	Meat	Food Pairings Ideas	Cooking Methods
MEAT, FISH, EGGS AND EQUIVALENT	**Beef** Ribeye Sirloin Tenderloin Chuck Brisket Rump Steak	Potatoes, root vegetables, mushrooms, red wine sauces, rice, barley, pasta.	**Quick Cooking** Grilling, Searing, Broiling, Sautéing (tender cuts). **Long Cooking** Braising, Roasting, Slow-cooking (tougher cuts).
	Pork Pork Chops Tenderloin Belly Shoulder Ribs	Apples, cabbage, sweet potatoes, mustard sauces, beans.	**Quick Cooking** Grilling, Sautéing, Pan-frying. **Long Cooking** Roasting, Braising, Smoking, Slow-cooking (fatty or tough cuts).
	Lamb Cutlet Chops Frenched Chops Loin Chops Leg Shoulder Rack of Lamb Shanks	Garlic, rosemary, mint, lemon, curry, couscous, quinoa, roasted vegetables.	**Quick Cooking** Grilling, Broiling, Searing (chops, rack). Medium Cooking: Roasting (leg). **Long Cooking** Braising, Stewing, Slow-cooking (shoulder, shanks).
	Poultry Chicken (Whole, Mince, Sausage, Breast, Thighs, Drumsticks, tenderloins). Turkey (sausage, breast) Duck (sausage, legs, breast)	Citrus, fresh herbs, garlic, honey, rice, quinoa, stuffing, curry.	**Quick Cooking** Grilling, Sautéing, Pan-Frying **Medium Cooking** Roasting (whole bird, drumsticks) **Long Cooking** Braising, Stewing, Slow-cooking (drumsticks, whole-bird)
	Game Meat Venison, Rabbit, Wild Boar, Kangaroo.	Juniper berries, red wine, garlic, root vegetables, curry potatoes, barley, wild rice.	**Quick Cooking** Grilling, Searing, Pan-frying (Steaks) **Medium Cooking** Roasting (Leg, shoulder) **Long Cooking:** Braising, Stewing, Slow-cooking (chuck, diced)

MEAT, FISH, EGGS AND EQUIVALENT

Fish	Food Pairings Ideas	Cooking Methods
Fish		
Barramundi	Dill, lemongrass, jasmine rice, zucchini, asparagus	Pan-seared
Blue grenadier (Hoki)	Chives, thyme, mashed potatoes, green beans, carrots	Baked, pan-fried, broiled
Flathead	Lemon myrtle, black pepper, polenta, slaw, broccoli	Pan-seared, grilled
Garfish	Basil, lemon zest, rice noodles, cucumber, fennel	Fried
King George Whiting	Dill, lemon balm, couscous, peas, baby carrots	Grilled, pan-seared
Snapper	Coriander, ginger, quinoa, bok choy, sweet potato	Pan-seared
Whiting	Tarragon, parsley, brown rice, lettuce, pea shoots	Fried, grilled
Medium-Fat Fish		
Coral Trout	Ginger, coriander, brown rice, Asian greens, pumpkin	Baked, pan-fried, grilled, steamed, poached
John Dory	Dill, bay leaf, new potatoes, mushrooms, leeks	Baked, pan-fried, grilled
Monkfish	Paprika, saffron, wild rice, tomato, zucchini	Baked, fried
Mulloway	Fennel, curry leaves, pasta, cabbage, cauliflower	Baked, grilled, pan-fried, steamed, poached
Silver Perch	Chives, garlic, couscous, spinach, corn	Baked, fried, grilled, pan-fried, steamed
Trevally	Coriander, lime zest, sourdough, broccolini, baby corn	Baked, pan-fried
Fatty-Fish		
Australian Salmon	Dill, mustard seed, rice, beetroot, roasted carrots	Grilled, pan-fried, smoked, baked
Blue Mackerel	Oregano, garlic, couscous, capsicum, kale	Grilled, pan-fried, baked
Salmon	Basil, lemon pepper, wild rice, asparagus, fennel	Grilled, pan-fried, baked, poached, smoked
Sardines	Thyme, chili flakes, toast, tomato, zucchini	Grilled, pan-fried, baked, barbecued, steamed
Tuna (Bluefin, Yellowfin)	Sesame, soy, sushi rice, cucumber, pickled ginger	Seared, grilled, pan-fried, baked
Yellowtail Kingfish	Ginger, lime, noodles, pak choy, spring onion	Grilled, pan-fried, baked, barbecued
Other Seafood		
Balmain Bug	Garlic butter, lemon, herbs, rice, asparagus, snow peas	Grilled, pan or stir-fried, barbecued, steamed, poached
Calamari/Squid	Lemon, garlic, chili, fried vegetables, cherry tomatoes	Grilled, pan or deep-fried, barbecued, steamed, poached
Crab	Butter, lemon, dill, potatoes, corn	Grilled, pan-fried, barbecued, steamed, poached
Lobster	Lemon, tarragon, pasta, boiled potatoes, asparagus	Grilled, pan-fried, barbecued, steamed, poached
Moreton Bay Bug	Garlic butter, citrus, fresh herbs, rice, pasta, greens	Grilled, pan-fried, barbecued, steamed, poached
Mussels	White wine, garlic, parsley, fries, spinach	Grilled, pan-fried, barbecued, steamed, poached
Pippies	Garlic, chili, lemon, pasta, rice, side salad	Grilled, pan-fried, barbecued, steamed, poached
Prawns	Garlic, chili, lime, rice, pasta, stir-fried vegetables	Grilled, pan-fried, barbecued, steamed, poached
Scallops	Butter, garlic, white wine, pasta, risotto, spinach	Grilled, pan-fried, barbecued, steamed, poached
Yabbies	Garlic butter, lemon, dill, pasta, rice, green beans	Grilled, pan-fried, barbecued, steamed, poached

<table>
<tr><th rowspan="20">MEAT, FISH, EGGS AND EQUIVALENT</th><th>Pairing for Protein</th><th>Complete Protein</th><th>Cooking Methods</th></tr>
<tr><td>

Grains
Couscous + Chickpeas
Rice or pasta + Barley
Rice or pasta + Corn

Vegetables
Rice or pasta + Peas
Rice or pasta + Spinach

Legumes
Rice or pasta + Lentils
Rice or pasta + Black beans, other beans.

Soy Products
Rice or pasta + Edamame

Seeds /Nuts
Rice or pasta + Almonds
Rice or pasta + Peanuts
Rice or pasta + Cashews
Rice or pasta+ Pumpkin seeds

</td><td>

Eggs
Chicken
Quail

Soy Products
Edamame
Tofu
Tempeh

Grains
Quinoa

</td><td>

Cooking
Baked
Fried
Omelette
Poached
Scrambled
Soft-boiled

Cooking
Blanched, steamed
Pan-fry, deep-fry, stir-fry
Air-fry, crumb, or coat with tempura.

Cooking
Absorption (rice-cooker, saucepan)
Boil and simmer in saucepan. Add stock for flavour.

</td></tr>
</table>

GRAIN, PASTA, RICE, BREADS

Pasta, Rice

NON-GF

Pasta
White
Wholemeal
Multigrain
Shapes (penne, spirals, spaghetti, etc)
Fresh egg pasta
Filled pasta (raviolis, tortellinis)

GF

Pasta
Corn
Brown rice
Buckwheat
Rice
Quinoa
Chickpea/Lentil

Rice
White
Brown
Jasmine
Basmati
Arborio
Wild
Black

Other grains

NON-GF

Grains
Barley
Bulgur (wheat)
Couscous (regular, wholemeal)
Farro, Freekeh
Quinoa
Rye
Semolina (wheat)

GF

Grains
Amaranth
Buckwheat
Corn (including polenta and cornmeal)
Millet
Quinoa
Sorghum
Oats

Check for certified GF to avoid cross-contaminations

Breads

NON-GF

Breads
Barley bread
Brioche or enriched breads
Flatbreads (naan, pita, roti)
Multigrain bread
Rye bread (pumpernickel)
Sourdough
Spelt bread
White bread
Wholemeal / Wholewheat bread

GF

Breads
Buckwheat bread
Chickpea flour (socca)
Cornbread
Gluten-free multigrain (sorghum, teff, amaranth)
Millet bread
Quinoa bread
Rice bread

	Cheese	Milk and Yoghurt	Non-Dairy + CALCIUM
DAIRY, NON-DAIRY ALTERNATIVES	**Fresh Cheeses** Cottage Cheese Cream Cheese Feta (often considered fresh, though sometimes aged) Mozzarella Ricotta **Soft Cheeses** Brie Camembert Chevre (Goat Cheese) Mascarpone **Semi-Soft Cheeses** Havarti Monterey Jack Fontina Butterkäse **Hard Cheeses** Cheddar Gouda, Edam Parmesan Pecorino Romano **Blue** Gorgonzola Roquefort Stilton Danish Blue **Washed-Rind** Limburger Taleggio Époisses	**Traditional Yogurt** Regular Yogurt Greek Yogurt **Flavoured Yogurt** Plain with Fruit Fruit flavoured Vanilla, chocolate flavoured **Frozen Yogurt** Plain with Fruit Fruit flavoured Vanilla, chocolate flavoured **Cow's Milk** Whole, Reduced-Fat **Goat's Milk** Whole, Reduced-Fat **Lactose-Free Milk** Cow's Milk Plant-Based Milk **Powdered Milk** Whole or Skim **Condensed Milk** Sweetened Condensed Milk Evaporated Milk **Flavoured Milk** Chocolate Strawberry Vanilla	**Milk Alternatives + Ca** Almond Cashew Coconut Hemp Oat Rice Soy **Yogurt Alternatives + Ca** Almond Milk Yogurt Coconut Milk Yogurt Oat Milk Yogurt Soy Milk Yogurt Check for Calcium fortified Dairy Alternatives

HEALTHY FATS

| Plant Based Fats | Omega 3 sources | DHA sources |

Almonds
Whole Almonds
Almond Oil

Avocado
Whole Avocado
Avocado Oil

Canola Oil

Cashews
Whole Cashews
Cashew Oil

Coconut
Coconut Oil

Hazelnuts
Whole Hazelnuts
Hazelnut Oil

Macadamia Nuts
Whole Macadamia Nuts
Macadamia Oil

Olive Oil

Peanuts
Whole Peanuts
Peanut Oil

Sesame Oil
Sesame Seeds

Sunflower Oil
Sunflower Seeds

Whole foods
Chia Seeds
Flaxseeds
Hemp Seeds
Pumpkin Seeds
Soybeans
Spinach
Walnuts

Oils
Canola Oil
Flaxseed Oil
Hemp Oil
Perilla Oil
Soybean Oil
Walnut Oil

Whole foods
Fish (fatty)

Oils
Algae oil
DHA oil supplements

IRON RICH FOODS

Heme Iron/100g	Non-Heme Iron	RDI
Best absorbed	Vit C needed for absorption most food cooked or roasted	**Boys**
Clams (cooked) – 28 mg	Pumpkin seeds – 8.1 mg	0–6 months: 0.2 mg/day
Black pudding – 12–22 mg	Tofu – 5.4 mg	7–12 months: 11 mg/day
Liver (pork) – 18.9 mg	Cashew nuts – 6.7 mg	1–3 years: 9 mg/day
Chicken liver – 9.9 mg	Oats – 4.3 mg	4–8 years: 10 mg/day
Lamb liver – 6.9 mg	Lentils – 3.3 mg	9–13 years: 8 mg/day
Beef liver – 6.2–11 mg	Spinach – 3.6 mg	14–18 years: 11 mg/day
Mussels – 6.7 mg	Chickpeas – 2.9 mg	
Oysters – 6–10 mg	Quinoa – 2.8 mg	
Spleen (beef/lamb) – up to 22.8 mg	Amaranth – 3.5 mg	**Girls**
Kangaroo meat – 3.2–4.1 mg	Black beans – 2.1 mg	
Beef (lean) – 2.6–3.5 mg	Almonds – 3.7 mg	0–6 months: 0.2 mg/day
Venison – 3.4 mg	Molasses – 4.7 mg	7–12 months: 11 mg/day
Duck (dark meat) – 2.7 mg	Dark chocolate – 11.9 mg	1–3 years: 9 mg/day
Turkey (dark meat) – 2.3 mg	Potatoes – 1.9 mg	4–8 years: 10 mg/day
Lamb (leg, cooked) – 2.0–2.5 mg	Raisins – 1.9 mg	9–13 years: 8 mg/day
Sardines (canned) – 2.5 mg	Prunes – 1.0–1.6 mg	14–18 years: 15 mg/day
Chicken (dark meat) – 1.4–2.0 mg	Wholemeal bread – ~3.0 mg	
Goat meat – 3.0 mg	Fortified breakfast cereals – 4–14 mg (varies by brand)	
Pork (lean) – 1.0–1.2 mg	Egg yolk – ~0.4–0.6 mg	
Tuna (canned) – 1.0 mg		
Salmon (cooked) – 0.5–1.0 mg		
Egg yolk – 0.8–1.0 mg (partially heme)		
Sources FSANZ – NUTTAB, USDA		Recommended Daily Intake, NHMRC

COOKING METHODS

Microwaving

Uses electromagnetic waves to heat food quickly from the inside out. Ideal for reheating, steaming vegetables, or cooking ready meals with minimal effort.

Grilling

Cooks food under direct radiant heat (such as the top grill element in an oven). Ideal for toasting, melting cheese, or crisping foods like fish, tomatoes, or bacon.

Barbecuing

Cooks food over an open flame or hot coals, usually outdoors. Ideal for meats, veggie skewers, halloumi, and corn on the cob — adds a smoky flavour.

Pan-frying

Cooks food in a shallow layer of oil or fat in a frying pan. Ideal for quick-cooking proteins (like eggs, tofu, or chicken) and vegetables with crisp texture.

Steaming

Cooks food using steam from boiling water below. Preserves nutrients and delicate flavours. Ideal for fish, greens, dumplings, or soft vegetables.

Poaching

Gently simmers food in water or broth at a low temperature. Ideal for eggs, white fish, chicken breast, or fruit. Maintains moisture without added fat.

Boiling

Cooks food fully submerged in rapidly bubbling water. Ideal for pasta, potatoes, rice, and hard vegetables.

Braising

First sears food in fat, then slowly cooks it in a small amount of liquid. Ideal for tougher cuts of meat and root vegetables — results in rich, tender dishes.

Stewing

Similar to braising but with more liquid. Food is fully submerged and slow-cooked. Ideal for soups, casseroles, and comfort-style dishes.

Roasting

Cooks food in dry heat, usually in the oven. Ideal for meats, potatoes, root vegetables, and traybakes — helps achieve a crispy outside.

Air-frying

Uses rapid hot air circulation to mimic frying with little to no oil. Ideal for chips, veggie bites, fish fingers, or reheating crumbed food.

Toasting

Uses radiant heat to brown or crisp food, typically bread products. Ideal for toast, crumpets, or warming wraps and pitta.

www.ingramcontent.com/pod-product-compliance
Lightning Source LLC
Chambersburg PA
CBHW032008050726
47590CB00006B/2093